MY FIFTEEN MINUTES

love
Sybil Jason

MY FIFTEEN MINUTES

An
autobiography
of a child star
of the Golden Era
of Hollywood

by Sybil Jason,

*WITH BOBBY BREEN,
BORN IN TORONTO, ONTARIO.*

BearManor Media
2005

My Fifteen Minutes
© 2005 Sybil Jason
All rights reserved.

BORN, JACOBSON.
11 - 23 - 1927.
8 - 23 - 2011.

For information, address:

BearManor Media
P. O. Box 750
Boalsburg, PA 16827

bearmanormedia.com

Cover design by John Teehan

Typesetting and layout by John Teehan

Published in the USA by BearManor Media

ISBN—1-59393-023-2

Sybil Jason, 83, Child Actress And a Rival to Shirley Temple

NY Times 8-31-2011

By DANIEL E. SLOTNIK

Sybil Jason in 1936.

Sybil Jason, a cherubic child actress signed by Warner Brothers to compete with Shirley Temple in the 1930s, died on Aug. 23 at her home in Northridge, Calif. She was 83.

The cause was chronic obstructive pulmonary disease, her daughter, Toni Drake-Rossi, said.

Shirley Temple's wholesome films tugged at America's heart and purse strings during the Depression and earned 20th Century Fox a fortune. Jack Warner, one of the founders of Warner Brothers, did not want to miss the trend. After seeing Ms. Jason in the 1935 British film "Barnacle Bill," he signed her immediately.

Ms. Jason, a brunette pixie from South Africa who was five months older than Ms. Temple, starred in a string of Warner films that emulated the sensibility of her rival's. She cried at a variety of provocations in "Little Big Shot" (1935), sang with Al Jolson in "The Singing Kid" (1936) and starred alongside Pat O'Brien and Humphrey Bogart in

"The Great O'Malley" (1937). But Ms. Jason never drew crowds like Ms. Temple, and Warner Brothers let her contract expire.

Fox then signed her, and she appeared with Ms. Temple in "The Little Princess" (1939) and "The Blue Bird" (1940). Ms. Jason later maintained that Ms. Temple's mother, Gertrude, had insisted that the studio cut her most dramatic scenes in "Blue Bird" so that she would not outshine her daughter.

Nevertheless, Ms. Jason and Ms. Temple, who became Shirley Temple Black, remained friends until Ms. Jason's death, her daughter said.

Sybil Jason was born Sybil Jacobson in Cape Town on Nov. 23, 1927. She began dancing and doing impressions with her uncle Harry's orchestra in London in the early 1930s. A performance at the London Palladium led to her role in "Barnacle Bill."

Ms. Jason was attending school in South Africa when the United States entered World War II. After the war she returned to

California to teach drama and act in the theater.

In 1947 she married Anthony Drake, a writer for radio. He died in 2005.

In addition to her daughter, Ms. Jason is survived by a grandson.

Ms. Jason never forgot her brief movie career. She autographed photos and released a quarterly newsletter for her fan club until 2010, when arthritis made it too painful to continue.

Table of Contents

SEE PHOTOS PP. 112, 114, 117.
(SYBIL JASON AND
SHIRLEY TEMPLE.)

Foreword

Into each actor's life, if they have been fortunate enough to make a dent in Hollywood history, they will most likely be identified with one particular movie role or character for the rest of their lives. This can be either a blessing or a heartache. To be so closely cloned to a character can produce the stigma of typecasting, and turn a potentially creative career into a dead-end street. This happened to the actor Anthony Dexter who, in 1951, portrayed the central character in the movie *Valentino*. Much to Mr. Dexter's credit, he not only eerily resembled Rudolph Valentino, but seemed to grab the very essence and persona of the silent picture star. After the movie was released, he appeared in a number of undistinguished action and science fiction thrillers but, regardless of the many times he auditioned for more prestigious roles, the specter of the charismatic Rudolph Valentino was never farther away than his shadow. Anthony Dexter finally gave up and became a school teacher. Of course, there is the other side of the coin. Long after an actor's career has come to an end, if his character had been so endearing or emotionally charged, then it is likely that it will continue to live on in the minds and hearts of the public. In the dictionary, the words "blessing" and "heartache" are diametrically opposed to each other. "Blessing" is defined as giving thanks to or invoking happiness. Heartache is defined as grief or anguish.

Can these two words ever be combined in a simultaneous emotion? I believe it can because it happened to me. I was Warner Bros.' first child star under a long-term contract and was either starred or co-starred with some of Hollywood's greatest legends. I am very proud of my work done at Warners. However, if you do not subscribe to the cable station Turner Classic Movies, where my movies are shown today, I'm sure you would draw a blank if I tried to describe the name of my characters and the titles of my movies. On the other hand, just let me mention my role as the little cockney scullery maid, in the 20th Century-Fox movie *The Little Princess* (1939), and there is instant recognition, and more times than not they reach out to give me a big hug. Sometimes it's very startling when they start to cry just by recalling their emotional attachment to my little character. This reaction puzzled me for the longest time until very recently when a young lady in her early twenties put it so succinctly. She said, "I could relate to Becky because the poor thing was always so put-upon." When we're young, all of us, at one time or another, have felt "put-upon." This is the kind of encounter that invokes the previously mentioned blessing/heartache syndrome within me. I'm happy that my work in *The Little Princess* has had such a lasting impression, but I'm also sad because the bulk of my work at Warners has had such a limited exposure and therefore does not receive the same kind of kudos.

But I don't want to give the impression that I'm ungrateful for the role because Becky has largely been responsible for keeping my name alive in the annals of movie history and in the memories of film buffs. Still, deep down inside, I admit that I am still hoping that one day soon the television cable companies will invite TCM into many more homes because, without a doubt, the Ted Turner motion picture library collection contains some of the greatest work of your favorite stars.

From time to time, when I do lectures based on my career, it never fails that someone will ask me during the question-and-answer phase of the program whether I have written a book and...if not...why not?

There has never been an easy or logical answer to that question because I have always enjoyed the process of writing. I suppose the closest I've come within the realm of an explanation is that I have always been a fan of other stars' biographies, and they all have had such a plethora of experiences over a span of many years, that mine in comparison would be just a skinny version of theirs. After all, bar some exceptions, a child star's reign is notoriously short. Yet something inside of me kept tugging and nagging me, saying I was just making up excuses. Of course, I sorely resented these accusations and intrusions coming from my subconscious, and it certainly wasn't my idea of fun, but it just wouldn't go away. However, one morning I woke up feeling like the world had been lifted off my shoulders. Apparently, I had come to the conclusion that...okay...maybe I didn't have a career spanning decades, but what I *did* have, was a whole lot of interesting experiences with some of the greatest talents in the world.

Could that be so bad?

At last, I had cleared my first hurdle with the decision to write a book, but now I was faced with an even more important one. What precisely would be the concept of my book and where on earth would I start? I kind of chuckled self-consciously to myself about that last one—common sense, silly, tells one that everything starts from the beginning. But the beginning of what? An autobiography? A fictional novel based on the truth? A career autobiography? It's now hard to believe that I mulled this over for weeks; one day it dawned on me that I had the solution all the time.

In my lectures I had always leaned a bit heavily on my "behind the scenes" stories involving world-famous people, and the audiences never failed to be mesmerized by them. However, at that time, I had not consciously jump-started my memory to bring forth so many that are within the pages of this book.

I know from personal experience that when stars have told me their own stories about the people that they knew, I could never get my fill of them. Hopefully, you will feel the same way when reading the following chapters.

However, before that happens, I feel that it is essential that the reader familiarize themselves with my background to understand how all of these experiences were made possible, considering that the aforementioned beginning took place clear across the world.

The following will serve as a skeletal rundown of the beginnings of one child star of the thirties and her exciting walk down a very personal yellow brick road.

ACKNOWLEDGMENTS

So many of the people who inhabit this book and contributed to my life are no longer with us, but to them I will be eternally grateful. However, the journey does not end there. While writing this book, I was fortunate to have been surrounded by a banquet of encouragement and help from old and new friends, and, because of their emotional and specific support, the creation and the fruition of *My Fifteen Minutes* became a reality. To start off, my heartfelt thanks go to...

My dear husband of 57 years, Anthony Drake, and to our angel here on earth, our daughter, Toni Maryanna Rossi, and our grandson and son-in-law, respectfully, Daniel and Phillip Rossi. I thank them for their encouragement and especially their unending patience when, at times, I have been incommunicado while writing this book. For their specific help, big and small, I thank: Susan King of the *Los Angeles Times*; Greg Orr (grandson of Jack Warner); Ned Comstock, of the University of Southern California's theater and film library, for his continuous and valuable help; Richard May of Warner Bros.; author Richard Lamparski; Bonnie Schoonover, Leith Adams and Lisa Janney, and their crew at Warner Bros.; members of the various chapters of the Shirley Temple Fan Club, The Al Jolson Society, The Jeanette MacDonald Fan Club, and The Eddie Cantor Fan Club; Robert Osborne, for his lovely introductions to my films when shown on TCM; the late, Dan Tarnow, of The Jolson Society; producer and writer, Chet Dowling; Dave Greim; Vera Van Dyke, of the Netherlands; John Treasure, who has been in my corner for many years; Owens Pomeroy and Gene Leitner, cofounders of Old Time Radio in Maryland; author Alice Levin; and the many Brits in England: Stan and Val Ball, Pam and Ron Wright, Tony Farnfeld, Michael Gartside, and Joan and Pete Chambers; the British Film Institute; the late, Dame Wendy Hiller; Donald Haber, of the British Academy of Film and Television Arts (BAFTA); Eleanor Debus; Gary Bell; Mike Burstyn; Jim Cox; Delmar Watson; Edith Fellows; Gloria Jean; Roy Thorsen; Wayne Gudgel; author Sandra Grabman; Richard Halpern, entertainer extrordinare; The South African Consulate in Southern California; Charles Hopkins, senior archivist and head of presentations at UCLA; Barbara Brocolli, producer of the Bond films; Alexa Foreman and Darcy Hettrich, of Turner Classic Movies.

To Gary Heckman, affectionately known as Hecky, who convinced me after a hard try that a Sybil Jason Fan Club would appeal to many people. As President, he went ahead and formed the club and, much to my astonishment, it soon became The *International* Sybil Jason Fan Club. To our officers of that club, who continually roll up their sleeves to make it and the various banquets a success, kudos go to vice president, and dear friend, Ruth Pollack. And to Michael Fitzgerald, author and cofounder of the Jivin' Jacks and Jills, who was my bulldog of encouragement.

And I must give a special Thank You to Laura Wagner for not only putting me in touch with the publisher of my book, but also for the sensitivity used in her writings that reflect her obvious affection for all of us from the Golden Era.

And to the three of my very favorite friends, I am most grateful for their big hearts and big talent: Ann Rutherford, Joan Leslie and Bob Mauch.

Last, but certainly not least, thanks to the man who has an undying affection for those of us from the Golden Era of Hollywood, and proves it with his many publications, BEN OHMART. Thanks, dear Ben, for being a publisher and an editor straight from heaven, and for being the sensitive human being that you are.

Blessings to all of you.

– Sybil Jason, 2005

She is just as nice as she looks, my dear friend,
the multi-talented Joan Leslie.

A Bit About Me

I was born in Cape Town, South Africa to British-born parents and, although it was never said in so many words, I do believe that I may have been an "oops baby." Apart from the fact that my two sisters and one brother were respectively, fifteen, thirteen, and eleven-and-a-half years older than I, years later I learned that after my brother was born my mother had been warned that it would be life-threatening if she ever had another child. She was so weak after *my* birth that my sister, Anita, started tending to my every need. Fortunately for me, even though she was but thirteen herself, she never resented all the work a new baby entailed and loved me from the minute of my first wail. In fact, even after my mother fully recovered from the ordeal of my birth, what started out essentially as a temporary situation, ended up with Anita fully assuming the responsibility of my upbringing.

There were no actors in our family history but there was a great love of music. The radio in our home continually reverberated with the sounds of the classics and of the voices of the most popular modern singers of the time. Although she was not a learned pianist, my mother would sit down at the piano every day and play her favorite pieces and, on occasion, my father would sing me the songs of his favorite singer, Al Jolson. The piano was essentially there for my brother. He was taking piano lessons and would ultimately become a famous pianist, bandleader and an owner of a piano school in South Africa.

I started showing signs of musical talent when I was just eighteen months old. My family noticed that I would listen very intently to the music playing on the radio and when I heard a song that I particularly liked I would toddle over to the piano and play the melody perfectly with one finger. By the time I was two years old my interest in music had

1

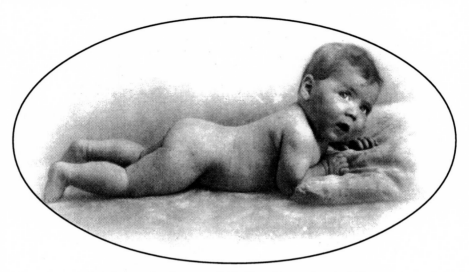

My first and only centerfold. Cape Town, South Africa.

accelerated to such a degree that my parents decided that although I was much too young to understand the intricacies of piano lessons, I just might manage dance lessons, for my sense of rhythm and balance were excellent. I must mention here that it was the norm for little South African girls to take dance lessons mainly for the purpose of learning grace of movement, but it was unheard of for a child of my tender years to be enrolled in a dance academy. Needless to say, the school was not exactly thrilled in taking me on as a student but after going through what amounted to an audition to see how well I could take instructions, they reluctantly re-lented and signed me on.

We little girls were taught ballet, tap, and acrobatics, and the ulti-mate goal of the teachers was to enter, individually, their most talented students in the Eistedford. In Europe and in South Africa, the Eistedford was what amounted to the Olympics of the Arts. To win in any category, one had to be very good and if one won first place it would be like receiv-ing a gold medal for the student, and a first-class reputation for the teacher. Initially my instructors never expected to enter their youngest pupil in this prestigious contest, but I had become so proficient in all of the dances that they not only entered me in all of the dance categories, but had high hopes that I would do well. I *did* do *very* well by winning two first-class places and one second place, in all three divisions.

My sister, Anita, was quite a remarkable person. Although not a singer or a dancer herself, when she took me for my dance lessons, she observed

This is what I became most famous for in South Africa, as well as later on in England: my Maurice Chevalier imitation. Cape Town, South Africa.

everything so closely that she was able, with expertise, to coach me in my routines when I practiced them at home. Later on when costumes were needed for our public performances and none were available in my tiny size, Anita, out of necessity and belief in my talents, became an absolute wizard at designing and sewing all of my intricate costumes. Our dance class had been together for about a year when our instructors started teaching us involved dance routines. When they thought we were ready, they offered our dance group to appear at various venues like festivals, benefits, town hall musical variety shows and in time we became a much-requested act. I obviously enjoyed myself so much while performing onstage that by the time I was four years old my teachers slowly started to feature me in the tap and acrobatic routines with the rest of the kids backing me up. I just couldn't seem to get my fill of entertaining and was soon supplementing my public performances with "living room recitals" for my family after dinner every night. They were all subjected to my latest dance steps and, for added measure, I started singing an endless repertoire of songs and musical comedy skits that I had learned myself by listening to the radio. It was not long before opportunity reared its head where my vocal abilities were concerned. We were practicing our new dance routine for a very important appearance and because our teachers wanted to "go all out" for the occasion, they were willing to hire a little girl vocalist to sing "Singin' in the Rain," which would precede our big production tap number. At break time, our teachers asked all the mothers if they knew of any little girl singers and, when nothing was forthcoming, my sister quietly suggested, "I think Sybil could sing that song." When they asked and received a sample of my singing abilities, they made the decision that I would sing "Singin' in the Rain," as well as head the tap number. Proudly, I became a hyphenated performer. I was now known as a singer-dancer!

My living room recitals were becoming a scene of discovery for Anita. One evening, I was relating a story one of my teachers had told us that day and, as I did, Anita doubled up with laughter when she saw how well I mimicked my teacher. That night, she got the idea that if I could mimic someone that well, why not imitate well-known entertainers? Anita started coaching me in how Maurice Chevalier, Mae West, Jimmy Durante and Greta Garbo sounded and acted when they entertained. Between those sessions, and hearing their actual voices when the radio played some of their latest records, it wasn't long before I was doing these imitations on stage and soon became as well known for my mimicry as I was for my singing and dancing.

One of my first ensemble dance numbers as Chico Marx. I did an acrobatic solo
dance number. Cape Town, South Africa.

It was obvious to everyone how very much I loved to entertain but
by the time I was four-and-a-half, my parents felt that it was time for me
to ease up on the show business aspect of my life and just enjoy being a
"normal little girl." However they were also wise enough to realize that, as
young as I was, to just stop all of my creative activities would be quite a
wrench for me. It would have to be something enticing enough to divert
my energies in another direction. After mulling it over for a while they felt
that a change in atmosphere would be a good solution to the problem, so
they made arrangements for Anita and I to go to England to visit our
grandmother, aunt and uncle, whom we had never met, and stay with
them for a month. The saying, "The best laid plans of mice and men"
certainly applied to us because our trip to London set into motion a series
of circumstances that set us on a journey that we couldn't have imagined
in our wildest dreams.

My days in London were full and happy. They were spent visiting the
London Zoo, watching the changing of the guard at Buckingham Palace,
playing in the snow, and getting properly spoiled by my grandmother.

We had been staying with our extended family for a couple of weeks
when one evening I felt comfortable enough to put on one of my living room
shows for them after dinner. It felt good to entertain but, after I finished my

I became a hyphenated entertainer by singing and dancing and heading the production number of "Singing in the Rain." Cape Town, South Africa.

performance, I was very disappointed because everyone was so quiet and had strange looks on their faces. However, I felt a lot better when my uncle went over to his piano and asked me to repeat a song that I had just sung.

Much to my delight, he accompanied me on the piano, and for the next few days I had fun learning the many new songs that he taught me. He was an excellent pianist and worked at night at the Savoy Hotel with the famous Mayfair orchestra. One evening on his night off, two of his lady friends came over to our home for dinner. They were both very nice and told some funny stories that even a little girl appreciated with great bursts of laughter. After dinner, when everyone had settled down in the

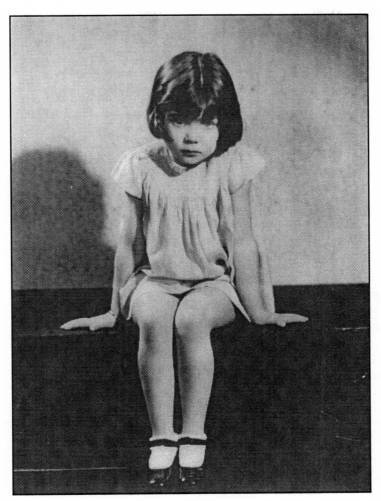

A test shot of me done by the London studio.

living room, my uncle asked our guests if they'd like me to entertain them. With good humor and amusement written on their faces, they said they would like that very much, so my uncle and I got to work. When we finished, the ladies applauded with great enthusiasm and asked me dozens of questions. Later on when it was time for me to go to bed, they both hugged me and said that they hoped to see me very soon. Little did we know that that would occur within the week.

Our guests were apparently impressed enough with my various talents to talk about me to some very influential show business leaders in the London community. Of course, when these two ladies talked, *everyone* listened. Because one just happened to be England's foremost entertainer,

Around this time I started playing the piano. My "loafing" days were coming to an end. Cape Town, South Africa.

actress-singer-comedienne, Gracie Fields, and the other was the leading chanteuse and recording artist of the day, Frances Day.

One gentleman immediately took them up on their recommendation. He was Andre Charlot, London's most famous impresario, who was in the midst of putting together a huge benefit show to be held at the London Palladium.

Miss Fields and Miss Day had made arrangements for me to audition for Mr. Charlot, and after I had sung a song, mimicked some famous stars, and played the piano for him, we were thrilled when he informed us that I would be added as a featured act in the Palladium show.

A fashionable sporty outfit taken at the London studio.

The greatest English stars of stage, screen, radio, and music hall (no television in those days) were all going to appear for this one night only and the scramble for tickets was tremendous and was soon sold out.

On the night of the gala, which was attended by royalty and London society, the international press was also on hand to cover the glamorous event, and some studio heads even had their cinema-photographers filming the show for posterity. It was a very exciting event and one that would not soon be forgotten by either the entertainers or the attendees.

When the reviews came out, they were very kind to me by saying I was an extremely talented baby and a real crowd pleaser. Almost immediately I was booked into appearing at the equally prestigious Royal Albert

My formal picture after having won the Eistedford for ballet in
my age category. Cape Town, South Africa.

Hall which in turn led to many other appearances at most of the top
theaters throughout the various districts of London.

Another thrill for me was to sing with Frances Day on a double-sided
record, accompanied by the London Mayfair orchestra. The most popular
side was a song called "My Kid's a Crooner" and, fortunate for me, the record
came out on the famous His Masters Voice label and became quite a hit.

It was hard to imagine how long Anita and I had been in England.
The time for us to have returned home had long passed and my uncle had
already written and received permission from our parents to stay a while
longer. Now *that* time had already gone by and my uncle, once again,

An advertising shot of me as Mae West for my appearance at the famous
Palladium in London.

found himself asking for another extension. With very mixed feelings, my
parents agreed that we could stay but only with the proviso that as soon as
things cooled down for me career-wise Anita and I were to come home
immediately. Being very realistic people, and judging from what they heard
about show business, they felt that the novelty of my talents would soon
wear off and we would return home to a normal kind of life. However, it
seems that I was soon going to experience a brand-new phase in my career, before I would ever see Cape Town again.

   In case it seems like my life was nothing but a continual round of
work, that assumption would be wrong. I was doing all the fun things

A more "exotic" shot of me as Mae West for my appearance at the
Palladium in London.

Me on the cover of the South African *Outspan*. This was an honor, like being on the cover of *Look* or *Life*! © Turner Entertainment Co., A Warner Bros. Entertainment Inc. Company. All Rights Reserved.

that were a part of most children's lives, and my sister and uncle had hired a tutor for me so that the beginning of my education would not be neglected. My teacher, who looked just like Ingrid Bergman, was quite an influence on me and because she made my lessons seem so much like fun, by the time I approached five years old I could read and write in both French and English.

One morning Anita received a phone call from Gracie Fields. She told my sister to get me down to London's Stoll studios immediately. It seemed that her husband, movie star Archie Pitt, was in the midst of filming his latest movie, *Barnacle Bill* for Butcher's Productions, and they needed a little girl for just one day's work. Even though I had never done movie work before, Miss Fields felt that I was more than capable of handling it. With those words of encouragement, Anita and I arrived at the studio where they photographed me, tested me on some simple line readings, and then hired me on the spot. The next morning I did my small part and then went home. We were very surprised when the studio called three days later. They told us that they had liked my work so much that

Barnacle Bill, filmed in London. My very first movie, with a first class English cast. Archie Pitt was the husband of Gracie Fields at the time.

In the main lounge of the famous ship, *Ile de France*, on our way from London to America. Anita is seated in the background.

they had enlarged my part and asked us to come down and get my new scenes which were going to be shot the following week. As much as I had enjoyed performing on the stage, I found that I adored acting in movies and told Anita that I hoped I could do that "forever and ever." Incredibly, a week after *Barnacle Bill* had been released, I was offered a part in a movie called *Dance Band*, that American film star and bandleader, Buddy Rogers, was about to shoot in England. It was not a big part but involved a scene very similar to the one Shirley Temple did when she sang "On the Good Ship Lollipop" in the movie *Bright Eyes* (1934). In my scene, which took place on a train, I strolled through the railway car in which Buddy Rogers' band was seated and, as I sang, they took out their instruments and accompanied me in my song—contrived, but very acceptable in the early thirties. I could not wait to make another movie, but for the very first time since I first stepped onto a stage in South Africa Lady Luck was not on my side. My sister and uncle were contacted by the legal council for the child labor board and informed that I would no longer be allowed to work in England in any capacity. In the early thirties, the child labor laws were very strict in Britain and the authorities were tenaciously zealous in protecting minors from exploitation. Our stay in London had finally come to an end and we started making preparations to go home. As young as I was, I was sad to leave England. I was going to miss my grandmother, aunt and uncle and all of the theatrical friends we had made. Worst of all was going to be the loss of performing and acting in movies. However, as Anita was in the process of booking our passage on the next ship sailing to Cape Town, she pointed out how exciting it was going to be to see our parents and siblings after almost a year away from home. I was beginning to feel a bit better.

It was still a week away from our departure when a hand-delivered letter came to us at our grandmother's home. It was from a Mr. Irving Asher who, at that time, was the head of London's Warner Bros. Studios. It seemed one of his cinema photographers had filmed the Palladium benefit show and when Mr. Asher saw my segment he sent a print of it to Jack Warner in Hollywood and asked the head of the studio if he could use a talent such as mine. After he and Hal Wallis viewed the print and decided I could be an asset to the studio, Mr. Warner cabled Mr. Asher: "Sign her"—and with those two words I became Warner Bros.' first child star under a long-term contract. With my parents stunned permission, Anita, my uncle and I left for America a few weeks later, aboard the famous French liner, the Ile de France.

The following years in Hollywood as a child star of the Golden Era was an exciting time, not the least of all this excitement was the honor of having worked with or knowing some of the world's most famous personalities. The following chapters will illustrate how very real these people were once they stepped down from the screen, stage, or newspaper headlines.

America the Beautiful

After leaving Southampton, England, at the very start of 1935, the French luxury liner, the Ile de France, sailed into New York harbor, and my uncle, sister and I got our first glimpse of America. What a thrill it had been to see the Statue of Liberty as so many other immigrants had before us, and felt the same awe they must have felt at the sight of that Great Lady in the bay.

After our ship docked into port and all of our papers were cleared by immigration, we were told that we were free to leave the ship. Although we had been informed before we left London that a Warner Bros. representative would meet us and escort us to the hotel where we would be staying for the few days we were scheduled to be in New York, we weren't quite sure what to expect. My sister and uncle (who now were my guardians) wondered how anyone was going to find us in the maze of people disembarking and disappearing into the congested throng of welcoming family and friends. We soon found out how thorough and mighty the Warner Bros. organization really was when a young gentleman approached us, introduced himself and whisked us away to a limousine while two other men saw to the transportation of our luggage. In the car, our escort made us feel very welcome during the ride to the hotel and, as we craned our necks to see out the limo window, he enthusiastically started pointing out the various famous buildings of New York. When we reached our destination, just like everything else, the pattern progressed like clockwork. After the hotel management greeted us, we were then escorted up to our suite of rooms where, within the half hour, our luggage arrived and were placed in the appropriate rooms. Flowers and fruit were everywhere and before leaving us to settle in, our Warner Bros. man made sure we were comfortable and told us that a table had been reserved for us in the hotel dining room for that evening. Almost as an afterthought, he handed us a schedule that we were to follow for the next few days. Most of the activities were for the purpose of our own enjoyment, like escorted trips to the zoo, visiting the Statue of Liberty, going to the Empire State building, and attending some radio shows. Very unobtrusively, and sandwiched in between all of the social activities, was a visit to the Warner Bros. corporate offices, where we were to meet some of the executives, a scheduled but unscripted radio interview for me at a local station, and, under a separate cover, we were handed a short script that I was to study for my appearance as guest star on the popular Rudy Vallee show, which at that time emanated from New York.

The four days spent in the Big Apple went by so fast that we could hardly believe when the time had come to leave for the west coast. As on our arrival, everything was taken care of for our departure by train, and after saying our "thank you's" and goodbyes to our genial escort, we settled down in our compartment for the three-day, two-night journey to Hollywood, California.

It was a fascinating trip. Anita had bought a simple little book that showed pictures of some of the cities we would be passing through, and also a map to track our progression from one coast to another.

As we watched state after state, town after town, disappear, we realized for the first time how very vast America was. We had short stopovers at several stations along the way but the one that appealed most to this five-year-old child was when we stopped in Albuquerque and I saw my first real live American Indian. I was thrilled when I was able to buy a little girl Indian doll, which I treasured for a very long time.

As our train sped on and the landscape became greener and greener, we knew it wouldn't be long before we reached the movie capital of the world, Hollywood, California.

It was just like in the movies. After our train had pulled into the station, we were met by a Warners' representative who handed Anita and I bouquets of flowers and a still cameraman who took pictures of our arrival.

It was a typically sunny California day and our escort, just like the one in New York, pointed out spots of interest on our way to the Knickerbocker Hotel. The Knickerbocker Hotel was almost always used as a temporary dwelling by Warners for their newly-arrived contract players and was located in the heart of Hollywood and only miles away from the studio. Amongst our fellow tenants was the devastatingly handsome Errol Flynn, who had been signed to Warners in London the very same time I was. Although I was never to work with Errol, our paths did cross occasionally across the years.

For the next two days Warners let us relax and get our bearings. It was a welcomed respite because, although very exciting, our schedule since our arrival in America had been nonstop and hectic. By the evening of the third day, we were ready for anything and it came in the form of a phone call from the studio. It had been arranged that the next morning a man would pick us up at eleven o'clock and take us on a tour of the studio, have lunch on the lot, and then have a very brief meeting with Mr. Jack Warner in his office.

We got all spruced up and awaited our carriage, which arrived on the dot of eleven o'clock. It was only a ten-minute ride to the studio, but what a thrill it was driving along Cahuenga Boulevard up to the crest of Barham Boulevard, to look down to see the unobstructed view of the tallest building, at that time, the Warner Bros. water tower, and all of the soundstages that were nestled in between.

We drove in through the front entrance, where we were flagged through the main gate by the studio guards, and then our driver deliberately drove slowly through the lot so that we could take in all the sights. Though we were quite familiar with the rather large London soundstages, we were absolutely awestruck by the sheer size of these gargantuan American ones. The exteriors were quite impressive, but the real eye-opener was when we were taken on the set of a Busby Berkeley musical production that was in progress. The set itself was not just merely an illusion of grandeur. It was as big and overwhelming as the finished product would seem when it was eventually seen up on the screen. We watched them do a couple of run-throughs of a production number but, because of some lighting difficulties, they did not shoot the sequence while we were there. (Unfortunately, I cannot remember the young man's name who acted as our tour guide but, for the purposes of identification, let's just call him Bill from now on.) Bill had been scheduled to introduce us to Mr. Berkeley, but the famous director was so deeply involved rearranging some of his dancers for better camera angles that it was thought best not to interrupt him while he worked.

Our next two stops were to see the facilities where the Warner Bros.' orchestra recorded background music for the studio's productions, and

"VIP" visitors to the set: photographer Guy Kibbee, and seated with me is his adorable adopted daughter Shirley Ann. © Turner Entertainment Co., A Warner Bros. Entertainment Inc. Company. All Rights Reserved.

then over to the Music Library.

The orchestra was not in session that day, so we had the opportunity to visit the miniature soundstage where all those recordings took place. We saw row upon row of chairs, each one of them with music stands in front of them, and facing the musicians was the podium where the conductor would direct them in the timing and interpretation of the action that he saw projected on the enormous screen that faced him. Behind the podium on the rear wall was the glassed-in booth where the experts did all their sound mixing and were the final authorities if a recording was good enough to use on the soundtrack. One only has to listen to the music from some of the vintage Warner Bros.' movies to realize how superb these musicians really were but, regardless of the musical miracles they produced time after time, most of them considered it "just their job."

A short walk from the sound studio was the Music Library where all the orchestrations and music sheets were kept. From floor to ceiling were wooden slots which housed the orchestrations, as well as copies of sheet music that were commercially sold in stores in order to popularize the songs in the most recent Warner musicals. It's wonderful to know that all this fantastic material was donated to the University of Southern California, preserving everything for future generations to study and admire.

When we left the Library, Bill pointed toward a two-story building which was next on our agenda. It was the men's and women's Wardrobe departments and as we approached the lower level we could see a line-up of men extras who were picking up cowboy hats, boots and jeans that were handed to them through a very large window. We didn't go inside their department, but instead climbed up some very steep steps to the second floor that housed the infinitely larger women's wardrobe department. As we entered the door, we took in the wondrous sight of row upon row of ladies sewing the glamorous wardrobes that ultimately would be worn by Warner Bros.' most glamorous stars. Just off of the main room was a little annex that contained dummies that were each labeled with the name of some of Hollywood's greatest legends. These stars would come in for their initial measurements, but after that the dummies, which were duplicated in exact size, were used for all the fittings except, of course, for the final one. Down a corridor in another section of the building was the office of Orry-Kelly, who was Warner's top designer, and just a few steps away we were shown a very elegant carpeted dressing room. It contained a chaise lounge, side-tables to match the décor, and a battery of huge mirrors. This was the room used when the stars came in for their initial measurements or their final wardrobe fittings.

Some of the nicest people on the lot came from the Wardrobe department. There was "Little Ida," who became my dresser on most of my movies when she wasn't busy with Bette Davis, and Kathryn, the supervisor of all the ladies who sewed the garments. Kathryn and the ladies knew how much I loved all the shiny and pretty materials and would spoil me by giving me remnants of them each time I visited with them.

When we left Wardrobe, Bill pointed to a grassy area which had a turnstile that led into the private tennis court and offices of Mr. Jack

Warner. We weren't due to see him for another hour and a half so we continued on with our tour which led us next to the Makeup department. We were very puzzled to see that it was practically deserted except for some technicians working on some wigs and a couple of starlets who were getting leg makeup applied for a publicity shoot. We were under the impression that this would probably be the busiest of all departments until Bill explained that the peak rush hours were between 5:00 and 9:00 A.M., when the ladies were due in for hair and makeup in order to be ready and on the set no later than 9:00 A.M. The department also had to be prepared to take care of the actors who had early morning location calls. In the case of the major stars, they usually had custom-made trailers right on the set, and were supplied with their favorite hair and makeup artists who catered to their every need.

When we left Makeup, Bill informed us that he was told not to take us to the Publicity department and when we asked why he said that very soon a meeting would be arranged and that it would be a long and extensive one. It would involve the discussion of my family background and the start of my professional life and how I should be introduced to the public in the most appealing and interesting way.

When we did ultimately have this meeting, the only problem foreseen by the publicity men was the subject of my first name. In 1935, Sybil was an uncommon name in America and they felt that somehow it could become a handicap. When the suggestion of changing my name came up, my guardians felt it would take away my identity and they weren't happy with that at all.

Publicity finally came up with a solution that pleased everyone. For my first few films, the scriptwriters would make sure that my character's name was Sybil and after it was used two or three times it would sound less "foreign" to the American ear.

We were fascinated by everything that we saw on our studio tour, but as Bill looked at his watch, he suggested that we have lunch in order not to be rushed for our meeting with Mr. Warner. There were two places one could eat on the Warners lot. There was the commissary, where most of the population ate, and then there was the Green Room (now called the Blue Room), where all the top stars, producers and directors could eat their meals in a calm and comparatively private atmosphere. On this day, all we did was peek into the Green Room, and then headed for lunch in the commissary. For a five-year-old child, the commissary was a place of

A publicity picture of me and Dickie Moore, circa 1935.

wonderment.

It was like walking into a fairytale book and becoming one of its characters. At each table sat an array of people who were dressed as cowboys, Indians, monsters, policemen, gangsters, chorus girls, and anything else that could possibly indulge one's imagination. I could barely eat my lunch because I was so mesmerized by my surroundings; it was hard to tear myself away from this child's paradise when it was time to leave for our meeting with Mr. Warner. Sadly, this was one of the last times I ate in the commissary because from then on we were delegated to eat in the Green Room. They told my guardians that, of course, we had the choice of where we wished to eat, but it was suggested very gently that the Green Room would be the more appropriate place for us to take our meals. We acquiesced to their suggestion.

I think that Anita, my uncle and I were a little nervous as we waited to see the head of the studio. However, all our fears were quickly dispelled as soon as we entered his private domain and saw a very genial man with a huge smile on his face arise from his desk to greet us. After shaking hands with my guardians, he put his hand on top of my head and asked me if I liked being in America. When I assured him that I thought it was wonderful that seemed to please him very much and he motioned for all of us to sit down. He enquired whether we had enjoyed our tour of the studio and if we were comfortable at the Knickerbocker Hotel. It really didn't seem like a business meeting at all until his intercom buzzed and he gave someone permission to enter his office. The gentleman that came in was a still cameraman and he was there specifically to take pictures of Mr. Warner and me.

They posed me in the chair behind his desk and told me to pretend to be signing a contract while Mr. Warner looked over my shoulder. After three or four pictures had been taken, the cameraman gave a slight nod and quietly left the office. We knew that our meeting had come to an end when Mr. Warner remained standing and told us that if there was anything that we needed to be sure to call the studio and it would be taken care of. He shook hands with Anita and my uncle, and put his hand gently on my shoulder. He told me that he was glad to have me at the studio and that soon they would be putting me to work on a movie.

We were all very relieved that the meeting had been so pleasant and as we left the studio to go back to the Knickerbocker, all that remained now was anticipating the time for my first assignment.

Little Big Shot

In my chapter on Mr. Jack Warner, I tell how my first movie was decided upon but for now, just let me say that the title of it was *Little Big Shot* and story-wise it was the mirror image of Shirley Temple's *Little Miss Marker*. There is no doubt that this movie was made essentially to display my talents because they had me doing every conceivable thing in it. I sang, I danced, I mimicked, I cried, I displayed a comedic side, I registering heartbreaking pathos and all of this was wrapped up with a wonderful cast and topnotch production people.

Featured in the movie as the two con men who get stuck with my care after my father is shot to death was Robert Armstrong, of *King Kong* fame, and that adorable scene-stealer, Edward Everett Horton. The love interest for Bob Armstrong was the "hard-as-nails but with a heart of gold" gal played to perfection by Glenda Farrell. Also cast as the film heavies was the greatest ensemble of gangster-type character men that ever snarled their way across a movie screen. To name a few, there was J. Carrol Naish, Ward Bond, Marc Lawrence, Joseph Sawyer, and Jack LaRue.

We couldn't have asked for better production people—we had Michael Curtiz as our director (more about him in this chapter); cinema photographer, Tony Gaudio; scriptwriters, Jerry Wald and Julius J. Epstein; and songwriters, Mort Dixon and Allie Wrubel.

Years later most of these gentlemen went on to win Academy Awards in their respective fields, yet even as early as 1935 their genius was already apparent and I was lucky enough to have been the recipient of their priceless expertise and guidance.

When *Little Big Shot* was released, the majority of reviewers gave it a big thumb's up and were particularly kind to me. Even in Louella Parson's column, in which she first wrote about me preceding the release date of the

movie, she was very complimentary. She wrote: "A captivating young lady of five and a half is giving the Warner Bros.' lot the same thrill Shirley Temple gave the Fox company when she first appeared on the scene. Irving Asher saw her in London and sent tests to Hollywood. Her imitations of Mae West and Jimmy Durante won her the job of Warners' only child star. If Sybil does a Temple at the box office, well, she will wear satin and so will her bosses."

The VIP visitor on the set of *Little Big Shot* is Colleen Moore with Michael Curtiz looking on. © Turner Entertainment Co., A Warner Bros. Entertainment Inc. Company. All Rights Reserved.

The movie opened up in all of Warners' major theaters across the nation, but the studio was particularly happy when its engagement at New York's 6,000-seater Roxy Theater was extended due to brisk business. The Roxy management even booked in a first-class stage presentation that starred none other than Ed Sullivan in person with his Dawn Patrol Review. Also on the regular program of feature acts was the famous tap dancer Peg Leg Bates. Taking everything into consideration, this was an auspicious start for the "new kid in town."

Michael Curtiz was probably one of my very favorite directors but, as brilliant as he was, he was a mass of contradictions. Quick to temper one moment and yet very gentle and understanding in the next, I could see, young as I was, how very difficult it was for the adult actors to handle. But handle it they did, for they realized that the results of his direction usually produced excellent acting performances.

Amongst other things, Curtiz was also a stickler for realism and substitutions of any kind tended to frustrate him. In the scenario of *Little Big Shot*, there is a section where a judge orders that my character be taken

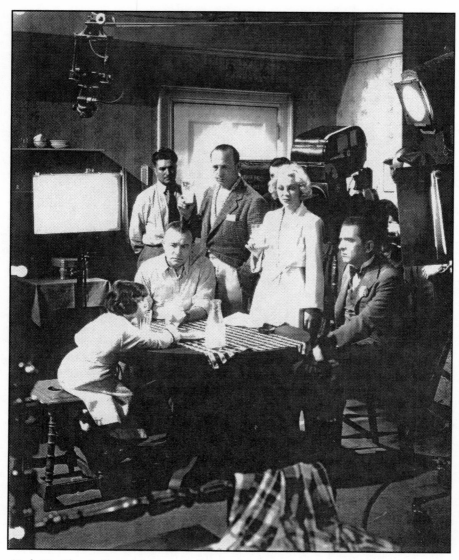

Little Big Shot. Left to right: me, Robert Armstrong, Michael Curtiz, Glenda Farrell, Edward Everett Horton. © Turner Entertainment Co., A Warner Bros. Entertainment Inc. Company. All Rights Reserved.

away from the two con men and then placed in an orphanage. In the scene that supposedly takes place on the orphanage playground, I am seated at a toy piano and sing a song to make me and my fellow orphans feel a little less sad and lonely. This was scheduled to be shot at the studio, but our director would have none of it and insisted that it be shot at a real orphanage. After much wrangling with the front office, they finally consented to his "request" and a week later we found ourselves on the grounds of the L.A. Orphanage.

The scene was all set up and as I sat at the toy piano, Curtiz carefully arranged a group of little girl actresses dressed as orphans around me. Almost as an afterthought, and at the same time satisfying his compulsion for realism, he posed some real orphans in the background.

Our first take went very well, but right in the middle of my song we heard the word "Cut." It seemed that one of the real orphans had moved in closer to the scene, which took the focus away from the central character and broke the drama of the moment. After warning the little girl not to move again, but to stay very still, Curtiz then ordered another take. This time it looked like a good one until we heard a harsher "Cut" booming out from our director. The same little girl had moved again and this time Curtiz barely contained the anger he was feeling. I looked around to see who he was yelling at and saw a sweet little girl with the biggest, saddest eyes. Right now, they expressed great fear and one could see that she felt that somehow she had done something very bad. It turned out that she had been so mesmerized with what I was doing in the scene that, unconsciously, she had moved in closer to get a better look. With great restraint, the director warned her for the last time and we then prepared for our third take.

Anyone who has ever worked for Mike Curtiz will tell you that when he lost his temper, it was a sight to behold. The veins in his forehead and temples stuck out, his eyes got a wild look and his voice got loud and hysterical. All of this happened when that poor child moved ever so slightly once again. This time she was so scared that she raced away from the scene and ran to the swings and slide area situated on the other side of the playground.

For those of you who are not familiar with all of the various jobs that people do on a movie set, let me explain why it is of the utmost importance to have a still cameraman there at all times. For the most part, movies are not shot in sequence but, if at all possible, they try to schedule all the scenes that take place on one particular set to be shot around the same time period. The most important job of the still cameraman is to take a photograph at the end of every scene for purposes of match-up. For a multitude of reasons, sometimes it is necessary, days or weeks later, to re-shoot a scene and if the actor's hair is disheveled or they have a smudge on their face, it is crucial that these things are duplicated the second time around. In the case of our scene on the orphanage playground, the third take, which did not include the little orphan girl, was a good one and at the end of the scene, the cameraman took his photograph.

Now let's front forward to March 1972. I was reading the then-popular Hollywood newspaper, *The Hollywood Independent*, and turned to the entertainment section. In the movie column written by Noble "Kid" Chissel, he was asking people in the movie industry to appear as guest stars in an Easter Parade. Initially he got a fairly good response from a number of stars, but when the place where the parade was going to be located was published, everyone pulled out of their commitment. Mr. Chissel stated that a lot of kids were going to be very disappointed if no celebrities turned up for the event, so once again he pleaded that the stars donate their time for a good cause. I have always loved children and felt bad that because the parade was not going to take place in an "acceptable" part of the city, they wouldn't get to see any screen personalities.

I had not made a movie in years, but a lot of my old ones were being shown on our local TV stations and from time to time I would appear as a guest with the TV host at break time and discuss the making of that particular movie. I decided to phone Mr. Chissel at the newspaper and explain who I was and that if he wanted me for the parade I was willing and able. I was prepared to give him an explanation of my screen back-ground, but as soon as I mentioned my name he practically exploded with excitement. He told me that he had known me since I was five years old and that he had been an extra in one of my scenes in *Little Big Shot*. Later on I found out that Kid was a mainstay extra at Warners and then later at other studios and had appeared in hundreds of movies. It seems that ev-eryone in Hollywood knew Noble "Kid" Chissel and valued him as a loyal and honest man. He really didn't want to wait until the day of the parade to meet me, so we made arrangements for our reunion for the next day. He was very sweet and told my husband and myself some fascinating stories about the stars and directors he had worked with, and even told me a few things that happened on the set of *Little Big Shot*. It was a meet-ing that we all enjoyed and agreed that after the Easter Parade we would definitely keep in touch with each other. We did up until the day Kid died.

In the 1980's, my husband Tony, our daughter Toni, and myself had a home in Studio City, and on our grounds we had a wonderful little theater we had built ourselves from our three-car garage. Many great memories were formed there. It was where we ran the movies of our friends who were stars, had wonderful parties and even put on plays for our own amusement. I sometimes taught drama classes there, and my husband, who is a wonderful artist, created some of his finest paintings in that ideal atmosphere.

One evening, Kid came over to our house for dinner and afterwards we started talking about the old days. I brought out a few albums that contained some of the hundreds of stills that I have in my collection, and that spurred Kid into relating some fascinating stories of the past. When we came to the album marked *Little Big Shot*, he was disappointed that he wasn't pictured in any of them.

When I inquired which scene he appeared in, he told me that it had been a street sequence where Robert Armstrong was selling phony watches and Edward Everett Horton and I were pretending to be customers. In 1935, Big Little Books put out a series of small books that featured recent movies. The books contained a full-length scenario of the story line and page after page contained stills from the movie. These fat little books became very popular and now, at the present time, they are sought-after collectibles by movie buffs and Hollywood historians.

Big Little Books put one out on me called *Little Big Shot* and that evening I went to get my copy because I knew that it contained several street scenes. We came across one that pictured Robert Armstrong giving his "spiel" and Everett Horton holding me in his arms while a crowd was gathered around us. But, once again, no picture of Kid.

(A few years later, I was fortunate enough to obtain a print of the movie and there, in that same scene peeking over someone's shoulder was the distinctive face of Noble "Kid" Chissel.)

We went back to viewing the stills from *Little Big Shot*, and Kid seemed to be particularly interested in a photo that was taken at the orphanage. He asked me where it had been shot. One must take into account that an extra is usually used only once in a particular scene in a movie, so that explains why he wasn't familiar with the orphanage sequence. After I told him that we went on location to the L.A. Orphanage, it seemed very important to him that I verify what year we had made the movie. When I reminded him that it was 1935, he got very excited and asked for a magnifying glass. Very puzzled, I got one for him and after he viewed the photo more closely he seemed satisfied that he recognized someone that he knew in it.

Kid had a very good friend who was a Hollywood writer-producer and, in the late 40's, they both became acquainted with a young lady who had dreams of becoming a movie star. The three of them became very close and the two men tried to help her out in any way that they could. Having been in the business for so many years, Kid saw many young hopefuls come and go and he told me that although he didn't see any star material in their new young friend, they found her to be very sweet and endearing in her hopes for a movie career. She had very few possessions but valued what she did have and proudly displayed some snapshots of her family and of herself when she was very young.

I still think back to that evening when Kid studied the orphanage picture so carefully. It was the one taken by our still photographer at the end of our final successful take. It showed me at the toy piano with the little girl actresses surrounding me and, off in the distance, one could also see three young girls playing on the playground equipment. To me, looking closely at that picture, I could not see any one child's facial features sufficiently in focus to make any kind of identification. However, judging by the outline of the body and the shape and texture of hair, and if one was specifically looking for these kind of features, it is quite likely that that one little girl was the scared little orphan who ran out of the scene. Eerily, that was the child that Kid pointed to as someone he recognized from a snapshot shown to him years ago. If he was right, and there is no reason to doubt his word, there are two factors that back him up in his assumption. The year that this took place was right on the button and so was the location of this event.

The little orphan girl he pointed to with no hesitation was the same young lady that he and writer-producer Bob Slatzer befriended in the late forties. As it turned out, there is a mighty good chance that in 1935 Michael Curtiz, if very briefly, was that little orphan girl's first director long before she was ever known as the very glamorous Marilyn Monroe.

Me And My Shadow

In 1936, I had been under contract to Warners for about a year and a half and they'd been very busy years for me. I had already made *Little Big Shot, I Found Stella Parish, The Captain's Kid, The Changing of the Guard, The Littlest Diplomat* and had recently finished co-starring with the legendary Al Jolson in *The Singing Kid.*

It is generally believed that after an actor finishes doing a movie, they then can relax until they are scheduled to do another one. Well, I don't know how it was at the other major studios, but at Warner Bros., adults and children alike were always kept busy doing a multitude of things when they were in between pictures.

For instance, I don't ever remember *not* working on my birthdays or on major holidays like Christmas and Thanksgiving, and all Warner people were expected to attend the local previews of the studio's productions whether one was in them or not. I can remember that my "leisure time" was often filled doing radio shows, benefits, appearing at department stores like the May company or the Broadway, where they were featuring Sybil Jason dresses and bathing suits. I even cut a Decca album of records on which I sang songs from my movies and was accompanied by Victor Young and his orchestra. If it sounds like I'm complaining about having to do all these things, I am not. Most of the extracurricular activities were really not so bad in comparison to some other jobs I could name.

If an actor was considered a star or, at the very least, a featured player, during the summer months when production usually slowed down, they were expected to go on a personal appearance tour to hype their latest movie and this could take up to six long weeks.

Then, of course, on the lot there was always the inevitable session with the studio still photographer. There were different versions of these

The Singing Kid, 1936 at Franklin Canyon for the wharf scene. Jolson, Alan Jenkins, E.E. Horton and me. © Turner Entertainment Co., A Warner Bros. Entertainment Inc. Company. All Rights Reserved.

This publicity photo was deemed "indecent" by the authorities and Warners ordered to drop it from all public media. © Turner Entertainment Co., A Warner Bros. Entertainment Inc. Company. All Rights Reserved.

Dickie Jones cutting into his birthday cake. Note: in the background David Holt is
observing us. Look closely near the top of my dress: a miniature badge that the L.A.
police made me when I was honorary captain of the L.A. police!

sessions and by far the easiest one was when you posed for an updated
portrait that the studio would use to send out in response to fan mail and
the media. As you can imagine, child actors did them more frequently
because their features were always changing.

However, child or adult, everyone dreaded the costumed holiday
shoots. These were the photos that showed you in the appropriate costume, pose and background representing the various holidays that occurred through the year. These were done way ahead of the actual holidays so that when the newspapers and movie magazines requested them
the publicity department had them on hand. These were really grueling
sessions and one of the main reasons for this was the weather.

I remember so clearly being dressed from head to toe in a woolen
snow suit, holding onto a sled, and standing in deep "snow" smiling away
at a gigantic "snowman." All during this session I was sweltering from the
summer heat and because of the hot studio lights it only exacerbated my
discomfort. One must also consider that no air conditioning or fans could

One of my stranger type publicity shots. I'm wearing one of the Sybil Jason line of bathing suits and dresses in this shot. © Turner Entertainment Co., A Warner Bros. Entertainment Inc. Company. All Rights Reserved.

be used for they could wreck a hairdo or blow clothing around, and everything must be still in still photography. To say the least, these sessions were nothing like taking family snapshots.

The subject had to stand or sit very still for an inordinate length of time while the photographer got the lighting just right. Sometimes, even after all of that, he might not be happy with the backdrop or the pose or even part of your costume, so time would be taken out to solve the problem and then you'd start all over again. In the summer we would shoot all the winter scenes and holidays depicting Halloween and Christmas and,

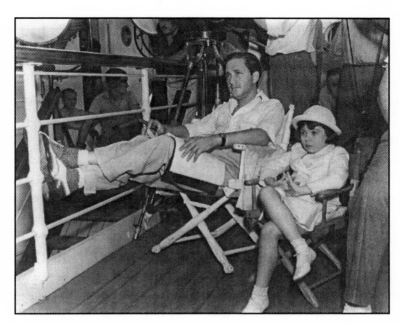

Movie making is serious business! Note my own tiny director's chair given to me on the set of *Little Big Shot*. On the set of *I Found Stella Parish*, 1935. © Turner Entertainment Co., A Warner Bros. Entertainment Inc. Company. All Rights Reserved.

My second movie, *I Found Stella Parish*. Left to right: Kay Francis, Ian Hunter, me and Paul Lukas. The first of two movies in which I portrayed Kay's daughter. © Turner Entertainment Co., A Warner Bros. Entertainment Inc. Company. All Rights Reserved.

in the opposite direction, in winter I was shown in all the appropriate places to have some summer fun like the park or the beach. One year they took an extraordinarily long time shooting me in Easter-type scenes such as riding a giant-sized prop rabbit and holding a basket full of highly colored Easter eggs. I remember wearing short, pretty summery pastel-colored dresses, and just freezing to death from the cold winds that always blew in Burbank in the winter months. Thankfully, those holiday shoots only took a week or two to do.

Now if one wants to talk about *really* hard work, then we'd have to turn to the subject of personal appearance tours. Personal appearance tours were planned by the studio as precisely as battle plans during wartime. Every moment and movement of the actor is accounted for. Traveling across country and stopping off in state after state, the celebrity would appear on stage in a theater that was showing their latest movie and perform some kind of an act for the audience. In my case, a master of ceremonies would ask pointed questions the public may have wanted to ask me themselves, and after that I would sing a song from one of my movies or recite a very dramatic monologue. On Saturdays, I did three shows. One would be in the morning, where the audience was mostly kids my age or older, then the afternoon matinee, and finally the evening show. In between the daytime shows, I was always scheduled to give interviews to the local press that usually took place in our hotel suite. I also made appearances at children's hospitals, orphanages, cut ribbons at the openings of department stores, paid visits to city halls to meet the mayors and receive a key to the city and in some cases, like San Francisco, to be made honorary mayor, and any other activity that the studio thought would enhance my popularity or my latest movie. That would keep any adult or child on a nonstop merry-go-round, but as a minor I still had to keep up with my schoolwork, which was handed to us before we left California, or to study a script, if I was scheduled to do a movie on our return home.

On the tour, we traveled to most of the major cities of America and, because I was British, Warners also included most of the provinces of Canada. As a matter of fact, in 1937 on the eve of the coronation in England, Canada made me their honorary princess. As exciting as most of this was, by the time we got back to Hollywood, my guardians and I were ready for a good long rest…unless of course I was scheduled to start another movie.

There was one aspect of being a child star in the thirties that was

The jacket of my Decca album of songs. The songs were backed by the wonderful Victor Young and his orchestra.

very frightening. Shirley Temple had been receiving kidnap threats and it wasn't too long before they started coming my way too. The law took this very seriously after checking up that this was not just a publicity stunt, and the very first thing that Warners did was to assign several of their studio police to a 24-hour watch on our home and issue me a bodyguard for all my public appearances.

I will briefly describe a part of my home, which will help to give you an idea of the tenseness we were feeling at that time.

It was a two-story Mediterranean-type structure that was situated on Sunset Boulevard. Right next door to us was the famous Ciro's nightclub and only a steep driveway separated our two buildings. Nowadays, Ciro's has become the Comedy Store and the property where my house sat is now the gigantic hotel complex The Hyatt Continental. At the present time, if you look up that steep driveway you'll see what is left of my property which is the garage and part of the maid's quarters.

My bedroom was on the second floor of the house and directly faced Sunset Boulevard. It gave me a magnificent view of the city, and at night the twinkling lights of L.A. seemed like a veritable fairy land. The bedroom itself was an extremely large room that had its own luxurious bathroom which was tiled and outfitted with gold-type faucets and accessories. Off the bedroom proper was another room which was the size of an average child's bedroom. The walls were all mirrored and were actually sliding doors that opened up to display all of my clothing. Between the actual bedroom and the closet room there was no door separation, and for a few weeks, if only in my mind, this proved to be a real nightmare for me.

During the day I could look out and see the Warner police patrolling our property and it soon became such a familiar sight that I would regularly wave to them and they would wave back to me. Nothing scary about that except that the normalcy would soon disappear once evening came. Our dinner hour, and the relaxing time afterwards, was pretty much the same as always but once my bedtime came, the nightmare would start for me.

Once I was tucked into bed, Anita would talk to me for a while or, if the next day was a work day, we'd go over lines, but once hugs and kisses were exchanged, my sister would turn out the light and close my door. There I'd be…alone in the dark with a very active imagination. Even though Anita had already explained why we had men guarding our home and assured me that there was nothing to be concerned about because we were being well cared for, I would lay there…dead still…my heart pounding, as I watched evil shadows lurking around in my closet room. I was sure that someone was hiding in there, just waiting to pounce out at me. In actuality, I was seeing different types of shadows that were caused by the police shining their flashlights up into the second floor areas of the house and bouncing off the mirrored closet doors. I never told my sister or my uncle how very scared I was because I didn't want them to think I was just a big baby, but I'm sure had they known, they would have immediately relocated me to one of our many bedrooms until it was no longer necessary for our home to be guarded. Needless to say, for once it was a relief to hear that soon we would be leaving to go on a personal appearance tour. I was still closely watched over and although we never had a bodyguard traveling with us, one was always assigned to me in each city that we visited.

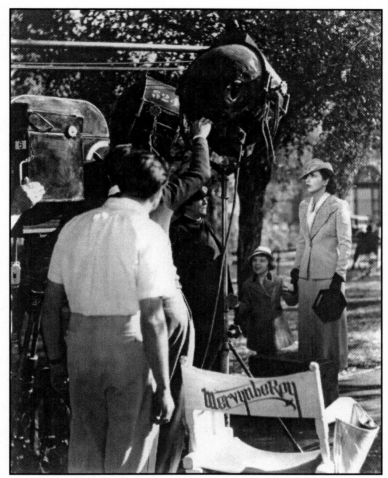

Mervyn Leroy taking note of our scene in *I Found Stella Parish*. Left to right: Jessie Ralph, me and Kay Francis. © Turner Entertainment Co., A Warner Bros. Entertainment Inc. Company. All Rights Reserved.

When we got to Cleveland, two very nice things happened to me. I think because our routine at home had been disrupted due to the kidnapping subject, my sister and uncle wanted to do something special for me. They told me that because I had been especially good, we could go hunting for a new puppy that we could take back home to keep my Scotty dog, Mr. McTavish, company in California.

Instead of the usual round of appointments attached to the tour, the three of us took off to go puppy hunting. I was one excited little girl, and it was so hard choosing the new pet because I just fell in love with all of them, but finally we all agreed upon the cutest little wire-haired puppy,

On the Santa Monica pier. This is my favorite picture taken with my beloved Scotty pup, Mr. McTavish, AKA Mac. © Turner Entertainment Co., A Warner Bros. Entertainment Inc. Company. All Rights Reserved.

who I immediately christened Peter for no particular reason except that I liked the name. I guess movie people were afforded extra privileges because much to my delight we were allowed to keep my puppy with us at every hotel we stayed at on the tour. One week before the tour ended, Peter was shipped off to California so that he'd be there waiting for us when we got back home.

The other nice thing that happened to me in Cleveland was the very nice man who acted as my bodyguard while we were there in that city. Usually these gentlemen were very serious types and very rarely spoke, but this one had a wonderful sense of humor and although he was quite reserved in manner, he didn't mind kidding around with me.

One of my assignments between stage appearances was to go to the Shaker Heights district and shovel the first spade of dirt at the site of the proposed new Warner Bros. theater. Along with the press, many VIP's attended the ceremony, which included various Warner Bros. executives, Cleveland's mayor Mr. Van Akin, and lots of civic and socialite personages. Right after the ceremony, and all the publicity pictures had been taken, Anita, my uncle and I, and my new but favorite bodyguard, left to go to the theater where I was appearing. Normally we would have gone back to the hotel, but the Shaker Heights ceremony had taken a chunk out of the morning so we headed for the theater where I was scheduled to appear.

When we got there, I still had quite a time before I was due to go on stage, so the Warners' representative informed the local press that they could interview me for a short while in the dressing room backstage.

As I sipped on a soft drink, the press asked me all the usual questions like how did I like their city, did I enjoy making movies, who was my favorite actor or actress. One of the gentlemen even asked me what I thought of my bodyguard, whom they all seemed to know quite well.

Although Americans and British share a common language, some of the expressions on both sides of the Pond mean completely different things, and this was hilariously demonstrated by my answer to their question about the gentleman sitting protectively by my side. To answer their question, I smiled at him and said that I thought that he was very, very homely! This brought about a huge wave of laughter and some very snide remarks directed, in a good-natured humorous way, toward my embarrassed bodyguard. Anita understood what had happened and quietly interceded on my behalf as well as his. She explained that to a Brit, homely described someone who was so nice that one immediately felt at home with them. I don't know if my bodyguard was more embarrassed by being called homely, or by the complimentary explanation of the word by Anita, but he quickly produced a large-sized badge and presented it to me. At that time he was Cleveland's Safety Director and this badge was part of his agency.

He was not long on speeches, but he did say that he hoped that every time I looked at the badge I would be reminded of my visit to their city. I have that badge to this day and I have never forgotten Cleveland or my very nice bodyguard...the real Eliot Ness.

1937, Cleveland, Ohio. Left to right: my bodyguard for a short while, the real Eliot Ness, me, and the Mayor of Cleveland, Van Akin. © Turner Entertainment Co., A Warner Bros. Entertainment Inc. Company. All Rights Reserved.

Turning the first shovel of dirt for a new Warner Theatre in Ohio. The fourth man to Eliot Ness's left is my uncle and next to him is Anita. © Turner Entertainment Co., A Warner Bros. Entertainment Inc. Company. All Rights Reserved.

From Sweaters To Sequins

Glamour. Mystery. Glitz. Pizzazz. For decades these were the words working around the clock to perpetuate this kind of image for their stars. In fact, during the thirties and forties, the stars themselves would never have thought of stepping one foot out in public without being carefully coiffed and groomed. They knew how essential it was to create the illusion of being special and most certainly worthy of being copied in both manner and dress by Miss or Mrs. "Average" America.

This phenomenon did not exclude the male stars from these essential trappings for stardom. Starting in the twenties, it was most desirable to assume the persona of the passionate lover, via the slicked-back continental look of Rudolph Valentino. After the release of his movie, *The Sheik*, American men diligently practiced looking into a woman's eyes with smoldering passion and even adopted a quasi-middle-eastern style of dress. Hollywood High School named their football team "The Sheiks" and for years had a huge mural painting of their logo on the side of the building that overlooked their football field.

By the thirties, there was a more realistic approach to mannerism and dress. It was a combination of a sophisticated and devil-may-care attitude that was done to a turn by such devastatingly handsome men as Errol Flynn and Cary Grant. This lasted up until 1951 when, in direct contrast, we reached the era of the tee shirt and jeans that Marlon Brando initiated in the movie *A Streetcar Named Desire*. The actor integrated this fashion into his personal lifestyle and the look still seems to be alive and well even now as we speak.

In the moral and upright society that we had in America in the thirties, there was one category in creating a star that was handled quite differently from all the rest.

As in life, the movies in that era had a black-and-white approach to the good girl/bad girl syndrome, and that was made quite clear by a woman's attitude, dialogue and wardrobe, and the studio made sure that one could never be confused for the other. For instance, the décolleté of their garment had to be on the subtle side or the eagle-eyed Hays Office would judge it immoral and refuse to give the movie its seal of approval. The Hays Office was specifically created to keep American movies moral, and insisted that any character in a motion picture who did not assume a lily-white and unrealistic image be made to get his comeuppance at the end of the movie.

The studios eventually found a formula that was acceptable to the Hays Office, and yet it was most decidedly sexual in nature. They came up with the brand-new category of a self-confident woman called the Glamour Girl.

This was the rage of the time, reaching its peak of popularity during World War II, when photographs of Betty Grable and Rita Hayworth decorated the lockers of GI Joes all over the world.

If you study the careers of these two stars, you will see that their metamorphosis did not occur overnight but was presented in acceptable degrees. The studios were very careful when grooming their contract players in this direction especially if the starlet was still in her teens. One always hears about star quality, yet no one yet has been able to define it. If that were possible, every person who was put under contract would have become a superstar. However, there are some perceptible directors, producers, and casting agents who have the ability to look at a young girl dressed in a sweater and saddle shoes and be able to envision a potentially glamorous box office winner. This happened to a "classmate" of mine.

In 1936, director-producer Mervyn LeRoy was assigned his next Warner movie. Jack Warner had bought the controversial novel *Death in the Deep South* by Ward Greene, which told of a Yankee school teacher who was accused of raping and murdering a teenaged girl, but in actuality was innocent of the crime. The major roles were already cast, but Mervyn was having a difficult time finding a girl who displayed a combination of girlish innocence yet exuded a healthy sex appeal.

The part was small, but very pivotal to the story, and although the director had auditioned many actresses for the role, none had come across with the image he had in mind. Finally, one day a fifteen-year-old unknown actress entered his office to be interviewed for the part, and, as soon as she stepped through the door, Mervyn LeRoy knew that he had found the girl

Publicity photo at one of my previews at WB Theatre in Hollywood. Warner CEOs are in the background. © Turner Entertainment Co., A Warner Bros. Entertainment Inc. Company. All Rights Reserved.

he was looking for. He was so convinced she had the potential to become a major star, he signed her to a personal contract. Before the movie actually went into production, LeRoy made two very important decisions. He changed the title of the movie from *Death in the Deep South* to *They Won't Forget*, and the other was to change the name of his starlet from Judy Turner to Lana Turner. In the movie, and much like the scene that Marilyn Monroe did in *Niagara* years later, when the camera focused in on her sexy walk, Lana made a distinct impression when, under Mervyn's orders, she dressed in a tightfitting sweater. He further enhanced this provocative display of her charms by making sure that the rhythm of the music used in that scene

In the Warner Bros. schoolhouse, writing to fellow pupil Lana Turner who used to pass me notes! Note arrow on wall: a picture of me with my Scotty dog. © Turner Entertainment Co., A Warner Bros. Entertainment Inc. Company. All Rights Reserved.

synchronized perfectly with the up-and-down motion of her breasts as she walked down the street. It's no wonder that after the movie was released, and much to her chagrin, for many years afterwards, Lana was known as the Sweater Girl. Although she was about to portray this very provocative character, Lana was still considered a minor and by law was required to attend school.

On the Warners' lot we had a schoolhouse that was unlike any public institution of education in the world. I guess the closest way to describe it would be to compare it to the small one-room schoolhouses that they had in the days of the early west.

Entering Warner Bros. schoolhouse. Note the French book under my arm. © Turner
Entertainment Co., A Warner Bros. Entertainment Inc. Company. All Rights Reserved.

Our particular school consisted of just one room plus a restroom and
depending on how many minors were working on the lot in various productions, the ages of the students could range, and did range, anywhere
from five to eighteen years old. Lois Horn was Warners' head teacher and
although she did teach at our schoolhouse, I always had her exclusively on
the set of all of my movies. She was not only my teacher, but became a close
personal friend to my sister and me.

When a child is working, the law requires them to put in a minimum
of three hours of schooling daily. The authorities didn't seem to mind that
it was done in increments just as long as the minimum hours were satisfied.

Of course when I was waiting for my next movie assignment to go into production, I was expected to put in full-time school hours either at the studio school or by my private tutor at home.

Besides myself, there were always the regulars on the lot like the Mauch twins (Billy and Bobby), who movie buffs will remember so well from the film *The Prince and the Pauper*. At other times we shared our communal classroom with other kid performers like Mickey Rooney, during the filming of the *A Midsummer Night's Dream*, and some of the younger members of the Dead End Kids and Lana Turner, to name a few.

Mickey always broke everyone up with his shenanigans and drove poor Lois Horn up the wall, but for the most part we all tended to our schoolwork. Naturally, we were all in different grades and our daily lessons were specifically designed individually for each of us. I was always the youngest one in the group but intellectually I was way ahead of the game because of my early induction into education when we lived in England. When I first came to America, as a foreign child, I had to be tested in order for the school authorities to determine what grade level I was capable of doing. To be a bit boastful, it was determined that at the age of five I was ready for the fifth grade, but ultimately the board of education felt that at my tender age, it might have a bad psychological effect on me, so I was not put in the fifth grade, but was advanced forward to a more appropriate grade level.

When it came to Math, French, and Geography, I did exceedingly well and sometimes was even capable of doing some of the work that the older kids were doing. Lana Turner was a darling girl but was never known to be cerebral in nature. She was excellent in Spanish, but generally did not do too well in other subjects. Her desk was right next to mine and, when Lois wasn't looking, Lana would slip me a note and ask if I could figure out her math problem. Funnily enough, sometimes I could but realistically when I just guessed at the answer and they would be wrong, Lois would ask Lana if she had received any help and then looked very pointedly and knowingly in my direction. I almost died of embarrassment, but my classmates just giggled and thought it was all very amusing.

It may sound like Lana lacked respect for our teacher, but that wasn't the case at all. She was just people-oriented and it was hard to discipline her or resist her bubbly *joi de vivre,* something I believe she retained most of her life regardless of the troubled times she faced in later years.

There was one amusing period when Lois Horn became very concerned with Lana's health. She even made it a point to ask Mildred Turner if her daughter had any urinary problems. Mildred assured her that Lana was perfectly healthy in every way, and that made Lois start to look for other reasons why her pupil would regularly have her hand raised to be excused to go to the restroom. The mystery was solved one morning when, strictly by accident, I needed to be excused not long after Lana's departure. As I entered the restroom, I was completely engulfed in a thick gray mist. Of course, it was just Lana puffing away like mad on a cigarette, and when she saw my jaw drop in amazement she immediately swore me to an oath of silence. I thought it was so neat that an older friend would rely on me to keep such a deep dark secret and even though I did, Lois eventually caught Lana in the act.

No one could ever figure out the strange friendship between Lana and me. Considering the difference in our ages, one would have thought that we'd have nothing in common, but for the short time she was at Warners and a bit afterwards, we certainly were good friends. As a matter of fact, Lois, Anita and Mildred Turner associated with each other on a regular basis in that time period and that is probably why no one thought it odd when Lana visited me quite regularly at my Sunset Boulevard home.

She was about seventeen by then and her visits usually consisted of spending some time socializing with the adults and then after awhile, and with their permission, Lana and I would leave to go to the famous Pig 'n Whistle restaurant located right next door to the Egyptian Theater on Hollywood Boulevard. It was always understood that, for safety's sake, Anita would call the restaurant one hour after we left to make sure we arrived there safely. It was also understood that the manager would call Anita when we left to say that we were on our way home. Even with all of this security, Lana still managed to make me her eight-year-old "beard"—and got away with it!

Directly across the street from my home was an apartment building called the Sunset Towers. This was probably the closest thing to what we nowadays would call a condominium because the tenants were rich and famous and opted to live in these luxurious apartments year round rather than in a house. Before Lana and I ever left for the Pig 'n Whistle we would scoot across the street to the Sunset Towers and take the elevator up to the penthouse. There, we were always greeted by a friendly, handsome man with graying hair, and obviously he and Lana knew each other quite well. He was very much the gentleman and always included me in their light and jovial conversations. And being the perfect host, would pour he and Lana a drink and bring me some coke in an heavy, elegant, crystal-cut glass.

His name was Greg Bautzer, a prominent attorney whose clientele consisted of the crPme de la crPme. Besides his bustling legal practice, he had the reputation of being the ultimate man about town and the preferred escort to the most glamorous women stars when they attended social or industry events. Although he had his pick of these sought-after ladies, none of them could get him to commit to taking the matrimonial plunge until a young Southern Rhodesian actress came along by the name of Dana Wynter and took him out of circulation. However, during the thirties, the attorney definitely played the field and Lana, young as she was, was one of the team players.

On our visits with Greg, it never failed that, after a decent lapse of time, I was told to make myself comfortable while they went into the "other room" to discuss business matters. They were never gone for longer than twenty minutes or so, but I couldn't help noticing that every time they emerged from the "conference room" they both had beautiful rosy complexions and wide smiles on their faces. In my innocence, I remember thinking to myself that those conferences must have gone very, very well.

After Mervyn LeRoy left Warner's to go to MGM, he took Lana with him and her reign as a glamorous superstar started to take root. I only saw her one more time after that and it took place at a charity event at Mary Pickford's estate, Pickfair.

By this time, Lana had a much glossier appearance and a decidedly sophisticated air about her, but, incongruously, the twinkling eyes and her famous giggle that I remembered so well still came bubbling uncontrollably out of her when she was amused by something.

In 1958, when I was visiting a friend in Bel Air, she told me that she must be Lana Turner's number one fan, but that she had never had the opportunity to meet her. I thought how much fun that would be if her dream was finally realized, so I decided to phone Mildred Turner first. We had not spoken in years and she was delighted to hear from me. When I finally told her what my mission was, she said that although Lana was at the present out of town she assured me that she would return my call once she got home. I never received that call because my childhood friend and her teenaged daughter were deeply involved in the violent death of the man Lana had been going with, the gangster-type, Johnny Stompanato, and consequently both their lives changed drastically after that tragic event.

I still like to think of Lana in the days when I knew her so well. The

Lana that was fun-loving, social and always the first one in a room to greet you with a smile and a big bear hug. Unfortunately, she is no longer with us but, thanks to her films that play regularly on television, she remains forever young and glamorous and I'm sure that's exactly the way she would have wanted to be remembered.

Oh Daddy!

1937 was a banner year for Warner Bros. For the very first time, they won the Best Picture Oscar for *The Life of Emile Zola,* which was also voted as one of the ten best films of the year by the *New York Times* and selected as best film of the year by the New York Film Critics. *The Life of Emile Zola* starred Warners' most prestigious actor, Paul Muni, in the title role, and although he was passed up for Best Actor, his co-player, Joseph Schildkraut won the Oscar for Best Supporting Actor. Rumor on the Warners lot had it that Muni lost the award because he and his wife did not play the Hollywood social scene. Although that may have been partially true, neither did Spencer Tracy who took the statuette home for his role in MGM's production of *Captains Courageous.*

Regardless of Muni's loss, Warners had won the top prize for Best Picture of the Year and the mood on the lot was humongously high starting from the rarified air of the Jack Warner office down to the messenger boys who made deliveries on their motorized Cushman scooter bikes.

In that same year, Warners released approximately 66 movies and although a good number of them were considered programmers, they also included quality productions such as the popular Mark Twain-based *The Prince and the Pauper,* starring my school chums, and still friends, twin brothers, Billy and Bobby Mauch, with Errol Flynn in the role as their mentor; Mervyn LeRoy's *They Won't Forget,* with fifteen-year-old Lana Turner making her screen debut; and *Black Legion,* starring Warner Bros.' workhorse, Humphrey Bogart.

I call Humphrey Bogart a workhorse with the deepest respect because if you look at his pictorial history at Warners before the year 1943, you will see, with minor exceptions, it suffered a severe case of the Yo-Yo syndrome. Take his billing credit in the 1932 production of *Three on a*

Test shot of me as a Mexican spitfire. I was supposed to have co-starred with Jimmy Cagney in a movie, but the producer hated the script and all the subsequent rewrites so the movie never happened, much to my regret. I would have loved working with Cagney!

Match, where he came in at a lowly 11th place, and then further dipped down to 12th in *Big City Blues*, which was released later that very same year.

Certainly one would have thought that his star would have taken a steady ascent after the 1936 release of *The Petrified Forest*, when the public and critics alike sat up and took notice of the actor who so brilliantly portrayed the psychotic gangster "Duke Mantee." which Bogart had originated on the Broadway stage. Inexplicably, it did not. What followed were, for the most part, lackluster roles. Being the complete professional that he was, he did his best with what was handed to him.

Humphrey Bogart, Frieda Inescourt, Pag O'Brien and myself. Bogie shoots Pat in the scene after this one. © Turner Entertainment Co., A Warner Bros. Entertainment Inc. Company. All Rights Reserved.

For a number of years he was delegated to movies that were routinely turned down by stars like Jimmy Cagney and George Raft, but in at least one case, it backfired on some of those first-choice actors and became a bonanza for Bogart. It was the 1941 movie, *High Sierra*, which both Paul Muni and George Raft vehemently turned down as a nothing script and a vacuous lead character, that turned it all around. Bogart took the role and ran with it.

If you will excuse the pun, I believe that Humphrey Bogart's strength lay in his stiff upper lip attitude and his wonderfully sardonic sense of humor. Whether this following story, credited to Bogart, is true or just apocryphal, it is so delicious and so *Bogart,* I am going to repeat it.

In 1938, the actor was being interviewed by a young reporter for a feature newspaper article, and one of the questions posed to him was what his next picture was going to be. He answered that in a few days' time he was scheduled to start production on a movie with Edward G. Robinson. The young lady had heard that to get an answer out of Bogart was like pulling teeth, but with the readiness of his last answer she was encouraged to ask the next one. When queried about the name of his next movie, with a very straight face Bogart replied "The Amazing Dr. Clitoris!" The reporter's pencil stopped midway on her pad and before she could react to the actor's comment, Bogart politely thanked her for coming and then left the dumbstruck scribe to let herself out. After the initial shock had worn off, the young lady phoned the studio the next day and found out that the movie's title was *The Amazing Dr. Clitterhouse*!

1936 had been a very busy year for me. I had already co-starred with Al Jolson in *The Singing Kid* and with Guy Kibbee in *The Captain's Kid*, wrapped up two of my four Technicolor shorts, and cut a Decca Sybil Jason Album, which was backed up by the marvelous Victor Young and his orchestra. Before the year was out, I got my next assignment.

The title of the move was *The Great O'Malley* and, besides myself, the cast consisted of Pat O'Brien as a dedicated by-the-book unyielding police officer, Ann Sheridan as my school teacher, Frieda Inescourt as my mother, and for the role of my father...Humphrey Bogart! At first my guardians were a bit taken aback with the casting of Bogart as my father

Interesting shot from an emotional "private" scene *The Great O'Malley*, but surrounded by the crew. Oscar-winning cinemaphotographer Ernie Haller is in the white shirt. © Turner Entertainment Co., A Warner Bros. Entertainment Inc. Company. All Rights Reserved.

Little Big Shot scene in front of the "theatre" doing my song and imitations. © Turner Entertainment Co., A Warner Bros. Entertainment Inc. Company. All Rights Reserved.

for a very legitimate reason. They both admired the actor very much but I still had a noticeable English accent and although it made sense that Frieda Inescourt, the Scottish-born actress with her impeccable speech patterns would play my mother, it was puzzling to say the least that Warners would choose their in-house gangster to portray my father. Father roles were not Bogie's forte and to make matters worse for him, in the credits I was billed above him.

The problem of the accents was solved when in the script one of the characters made mention that the Phillips family originally came from Canada but had emigrated to America in search of better job opportunities for the father and a better life for his wife and child. Of course, dramatically the writers made sure that the better life didn't come until nearly the end of the movie.

The Phillips family lived in a rundown part of town in a small dingy apartment. The father was out of work and his little daughter, Barbara, was crippled but there was no money available for an operation. Phillips finally gets a job and while driving his beat-up car on his way to his first day of work, O'Malley stops and cites him for a broken muffler. This ultimately makes the father late for work and his job is given to another man.

Through a set of circumstances, Phillips gets sent to jail but, known for his nit-picking, O'Malley's superior temporarily demotes him to a cop on the beat and, much to the amusement of his fellow officers, is assigned to escorting kids across the street to their school. Need I say more?

It was hinted that my favorite director, Michael Curtiz, who guided me so beautifully in *Little Big Shot*, would be the director, but, inexplicably, the assignment was given to German director, William Dieterle. I say inexplicably because we didn't find out until much later that the director did not want the *O'Malley* assignment. He had written an angry letter to Hal Wallis who, besides being a producer, was also co-executive in change of all Warner productions. Dieterle complained that Wallis had faulted on his promises that only Henry Blanke would be assigned to all of his movies, and that those movies would be credited as William Dieterle Productions. There was one more stipulation. He was never to be assigned to any gangster movies. Although this letter was delivered to the Wallis office, the executive was out of town and never read it, so very reluctantly William Dieterle prepared to start production of *The Great O'Malley*.

There is no doubt that he was a very good director. At Warners, in the thirties, some of his outstanding work was as co-director along with his mentor Max Reinhardt on the extravaganza *A Midsummer Night's Dream*, and full director on *The Story of Louis Pasteur*, *The Life of Emile Zola, Juarez,* and many other fine Warner productions. Some of his later work at other studios were just as prestigious, and included *The Hunchback of Notre Dame* (1939), *I'll Be Seeing You* (1945), *Portrait of Jennie* (1949), and *Elephant Walk* (1954). No doubt a most impressive directorial background, but it doesn't give one hint of the very complicated and demanding persona that was William Dieterle.

Mr. Dieterle and his wife were very much into the quasi-science of astrology and based most of their personal, as well as their business, decisions on the most favorable alignments of the stars. Our production was held up for a week because according to his astrological charts the best date to start was the following week.

Up until *The Great O'Malley*, every set that I had worked on had a friendly atmosphere and by the end of the shooting schedule cast and crew blended into a family-type feeling. Not so on the Dieterle set. From day one, our director was unresponsive, cold, and, except for his directo-

In between scenes of *The Great O'Malley*, 1937. Left to right: Bogart, O'Brien, Inescourt, Sheridan and Jason. Bogie was not happy that his "rest" time was taken up posing! © Turner Entertainment Co., A Warner Bros. Entertainment Inc. Company. All Rights Reserved.

rial duties, was uncommunicative toward his actors, especially the women. As young as I was, I could feel the underlying tension throughout the filming but at least two of our cast members seemed to take it all with a grain of salt. One was Ann Sheridan and, yes, you guessed it, the other was Bogie.

Annie was a fun-loving woman, a jokester, and had a heart of gold. Dieterle seemed to take a particular dislike to her because she had a loud and boisterous laugh that always reached its peak during shooting breaks and lunchtime.

One day we were shooting outdoors on the East Side of New York set, and midway through our lunch hour when Pat O'Brien, Bogie, Annie and I were sitting around munching on some sandwiches and having a fun and relaxing time, we were paid an unusual visit by our director who never socialized in between scenes.

He started telling us what he wanted to accomplish in the next scene

Break time off the set of *The Great O'Malley*. Ann Sheridan and I are posing with a watermelon that a fan sent me. It was judged the largest one grown in the USA.
© Turner Entertainment Co., A Warner Bros. Entertainment Inc. Company. All Rights Reserved.

but it was pointless because none of it applied to any of us actors but rather to his technicians. The adults finally figured out that Annie's laughter must have been bugging him more than usual and this was his way of watering down our fun. During his discourse, he temporarily turned his back on Ann and it was then she went into action and we had to rely on our best acting abilities not to break up.

You see, one of Dieterle's many idiosyncrasies was that he was never seen without wearing a massive pair of white gloves. Because of this, rumors circulated around Hollywood that he either suffered from some devastating disease like leprosy or had one humongous germ fetish. That day at lunchtime while his back was turned to Ann, she grabbed one of the electrician's gloves that were nearby, put it on her hand, and mugged outrageously while he talked to us. When I looked over at Bogart, his eyes were squinted and although he was not smiling somehow his teeth were bared. Pat's Irish eyes were twinkling away even though his mouth was expressionless and I knew I had to do something to keep from giggling so I dug my fingernails into my other hand. Mr. Dieterle must have sensed something because he quickly whirled around to face Ann just in time to see her drop the electrician's glove. Our director was not a stupid man. He gave her a look of disgust and walked away.

There were many upheavals of one kind or another during the making of *O'Malley*. Some of them were petty and others were downright cruel. The latter took place during the scene where Frieda Inescourt had to carry me across the squalid Phillips living room and deposit me gently upon a small couch. In order to give me the legitimate look of a crippled girl, a heavy steel cast was attached to the back of my leg so that it would always look stiff and unwieldy and, to keep it in place, wide strips of adhesive tape were wound around my leg. It never showed because, as a poor girl, I always wore heavy black stockings. For a few days we removed the steel cast at lunchtime to give my leg a rest, but it became so painful when they ripped off the tape, it was decided that from then on I would just keep it on all day and take it off after the work day was over.

The rehearsal of the living room sequence went well but it couldn't have been too much fun for Miss Inescourt. I was not a heavy child, but I was supposed to have been hurt and she had the burden of carrying my dead weight plus the weight of the heavy steel cast across the room and place me gently down on the couch.

Dieterle was satisfied that we were prepared enough to shoot it and he ordered the first take. I was placed in Miss Inescourt's arms, we smiled at each other encouragingly, and then started the scene. All went well until we got to the couch. It seemed like her arms just gave out, and I was dropped like a rock onto the couch. I wasn't hurt in any way, but I could tell that Miss Inescourt was just devastated by what happened, and, if the situation was not embarrassing enough for her, we heard Dieterle's voice boom out, "How could you be so stupid to drop the girl!" Being the lady that she was, she apologized and asked for a few minutes rest, after which she assured everyone that she would be able to do the scene over again. That dear lady did, but without ever telling anyone that, at the time, she was suffering with the beginnings of a very serious muscular disease from which she would finally succumbed many years later. I will never forget what a brave and classy lady she was.

There were a few other petty annoyances that we had to deal with and one of them involved me. There was a tradition in my family that all us daughters would wear a gold bangle on their hand from babyhood to twelve years old or so. If you look at all my stills, press clippings, and movies, you will see that bangle on my right hand.

In the first scene that we shot of *O'Malley*, William Dieterle spotted it and ordered us to get rid of it. My sister Anita was the gentlest of all souls, but when the director ordered the bracelet off my hand she stood her ground and told him how important it was to our family. Besides that, the bracelet would have to be cut off!! To go against anything that this director ordered was like waving a red flag in front of a bull's face!

They went back and forth on the problem and when it looked like it was going to be a stalemate, Humphrey Bogart, who always kept to himself, got fed up and snarled, "For Christ's sake, Bill, the kid coulda gotten the damn bracelet from a dime store. Let her wear it!" That was all that our director needed to hear. He got to the nearest telephone on the set and called Mr. Warner's office and demanded to speak to him. According to a crew member who overheard the heated conversation, Dieterle's side of the talk was rapid and vehement in nature, but evidently Mr. Warner must have felt the same way Bogie did because my bangle stayed on and nothing was ever mentioned about it again. I must say that my director's feelings were pretty clear when, at the end of the movie, I asked him to sign my autograph book that was filled with loving messages from some of the greatest legends in the world. He wrote "Fur Sybil Chason: Auf Wiedersehen. Dieterele." I guess that said it all!

I think the funniest things that happened on that set involved Humphrey Bogart. I believe the line he uttered a few years later in the legendary movie *Casablanca*, explains his seeming attitude of nothing is worth worrying about and, if it is, it probably "doesn't amount to a hill of beans!"

At that time in his personal life, Bogie was separated from his second wife, actress Mary Phillips, and dating another actress by the name of Mayo Methot, who he married a year later. One day, Miss Methot made a surprise visit to the set and what happened next was probably a foreshadowing of what would be aptly known as the "Battling Bogarts."

Miss Methot had apparently suspected her lover of philandering and she wanted to get a few things straight. The crew was busy preparing for a new set-up, so there was nothing much happening with us actors at that time. A number of people saw Miss Methot enter Mr. Bogart's trailer dressing room and it was not long after that we all heard sounds of things being smashed and saw the trailer violently rock back and forth. Needless to say, all eyes were glued on the trailer and before long we saw the door open and Bogie stepped out and calmly sat down on the nearest canvas chair and started to read a book. The destructive sounds continued to come from the trailer until, very abruptly, the door was shoved open and Miss Methot, with disarranged hair and hat askew, slammed it shut and stomped off the soundstage in a huff. A few minutes later, Bogie got up, entered his trailer and didn't emerge until he was needed on the set. Overnight, his trailer had to be refurbished because the blinds had been ripped down and anything breakable had been smashed to smithereens. It's a tribute to the tough guy Bogie that throughout their marriage he had been more than tolerant of her paranoia and temper tantrums brought on by heavy drinking, and even after their divorce he helped her out in many ways. Humphrey Bogart's persona may have been hard-as-a-rock, but apparently there was a tender side to the man that he did not easily display.

I think the most delicious Bogart coup de gras was the time when he and William Dieterle were having a disagreement on how a scene should be played. It was a very simple scene and ordinarily there would have been no need for a discussion between an actor and a director, but it was the great Dieterle, and, by now, a most fed-up-to-the-teeth actor!

I was not in this scene, but was sitting only a short distance away from the action doing my schoolwork. Their argument got to fever pitch until Bogie halted the conversation and said, "Okay, let's shoot it." Visually, you could see that the director was pleased that Bogart had come to his senses and finally saw it his way, so he gave the order, "CAMERA...ACTION."

My head was down into my school books when I heard an intake of breath coming from my teacher and I looked up just in time to see that Bogie had unzipped...exposed...and relieved himself on camera. He had a delightful grin on his face when our director went into the throes of an apoplectic fit and screamed, "What the hell do you think you are doing!!!!" Mr. Bogart calmly replied that he intended to do more of the same—or worse—until he could play the scene the way he felt was the best way...*his* way!

Of all the movies I ever made, I do believe that *The Great O'Malley* was for me, the most educational—to say the least!

Friends On Film...Friends In Life

In the 1930s, Warner Bros. was like a well-cogged wheel that continually churned out a product that America and the rest of the world clamored for. While watching those movies today, we discover that a good percentage of them have a quality and an appeal that holds-up in this era. This may partially explain why nostalgia sells big time.

I find it fascinating that the age of the movie buff keeps getting younger and younger and to hear a fourteen-year-old talk with authority about Al Jolson in *The Jazz Singer* and Bette Davis in *The Letter* and expel up-to-the-minute data on the stars who are still alive from the classic movie *Gone With the Wind* quite incongruous.

Throughout the year I am invited to be a guest at the various functions that honor those of us from the Golden Era for our past work. Without fail, there to greet us as we start to enter the hotel or theater are the movie buffs armed with their cameras and autograph books. I have been acquainted with a number of generations of them and have even managed to acknowledge some of them by their first names. They are a generous group of people who clue each other in on where and when the next celebrity event is to take place. They even offer rides to those who have no means of transportation.

Another nice aspect to these people that I have noticed is that the older buff assumes the role of mentor to the youngsters new to the game and patiently guides them through the best steps to take in order to approach a celebrity. There have been many times when one of the older pros will come up to me with a young person in tow and say, "Miss Jason, I'd like you to meet so and so, who is quite a fan of yours since he saw you in such-and-such a movie and would love to get your autograph or be able to take your picture."

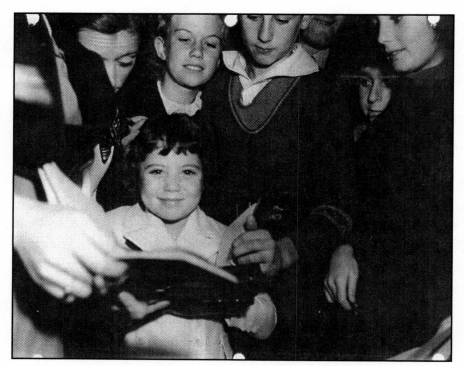

Signing autographs at one of my previews. That's Anita behind me with a wrinkled forehead. We both got nervous when separated by crowding fans. © Turner Entertainment Co., A Warner Bros. Entertainment Inc. Company. All Rights Reserved.

One cannot compare these polite people with the paparazzi of this era. Realistically, even though I'm sure there is swapping going on with our autographs or pictures by our movie buffs, the big difference is that they are genuinely interested in our past and not just for the sake of making a profit from our signatures or the pictures that they take of us. When I see the stars of this era being mauled and their privacy invaded by the paparazzi, I think back to the reporters and photographers of my day.

In the 1930's and 40's, most of the fourth-estaters worked for the major newspapers across the nation as well as the glossy movie magazines that were so popular in those eras. A lot of them were freelancers who earned their living selling interviews and photos on a piecemeal basis. Although they did not have the luxury of a regular paycheck, they could do quite well financially by selling interviews and unusual photos that no one else had.

I believe that the king of all freelance photographers was a man by the name of Hymie Fink. There wasn't a star who was not acquainted with

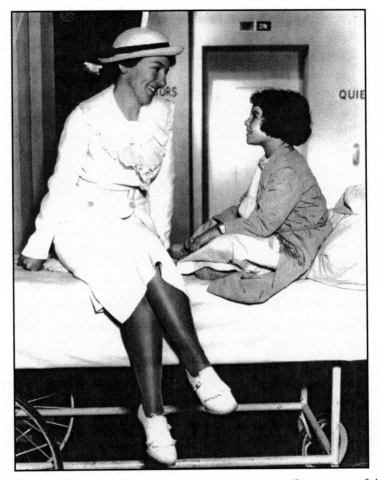

Fellow South African Nora Laing visiting me at Warners. She was one of the founders of the Foreign Press and the Golden Globes.

Hymie and would willingly pose for this quiet and polite man whenever they saw him covering any of their public or personal social dates. He looked very much like the well-known Hollywood columnist Sidney Skolsky, and Hymie probably had the largest collection of celebrity candid photos of anyone else.

The newspaper reporters and photographers of that era certainly earned the title of gentlemen and ladies of the press because they represented a true sense of professionalism which those of us in the limelight recognized and reciprocated with courtesy and respect. After all, they were largely responsible for the popularity we had with the public, and our studios and managers all recognized that fact. To a point, each major studio at that time had their own publicity department and one of their main duties was to send out news releases about their studio's top-rated stars, their up-and-coming stars in the making, and of the studios' new or future movie releases. Although the publicity department wooed the members of the press, they were quite zealous on the subject of letting outside reporters get onto the preferred list which allowed them, without supervision, to interview a star right on the movie lot.

I had been under contract to Warners for a little over a year when a woman reporter approached my sister at a benefit shoot that I was appearing in. She was a South African and was having no luck gaining entry onto the Warners lot to do an interview with me, and asked Anita if there was some way to she could help her. My sister said that she would try and, good as her word, Anita was responsible for Nora Laing getting on the preferred list at Warners and later onto the other studio lots as well. Until the day that she died, Nora continued to write feature stories about me for newspapers and magazines worldwide and ultimately became one of the founders of the Foreign Press Association. In this era when their Golden Globes extravaganza is held, many say that the winners of these awards are the precursors of the eventual outcome of the Oscar derby and this has proven to be more fact than fiction. From its very humble beginnings, the Golden Globes are taken very seriously by the actors and producers of Hollywood and has become as prestigious and glamorous as the Oscars have been for many years.

Of course, I am not saying that all of the fourth-estaters in the Golden Era were considered genteel. There were two women columnists that reigned supreme and, with the flick of a typewriter key, Louella Parsons and Hedda Hopper could demolish an actor's career or give a devastating review of a movie that some studio had invested millions in. Although Parsons and Hopper shared the same profession and power, the similarities end there.

Physically, Louella Parsons was on the short side, rather stout, and was quite a drinker. Except for the motion picture industry of which she was undeniably an expert, she was somewhat intellectually challenged on any other subject. On the other hand, Hedda Hopper was a tall and elegant-looking woman who at one time had been an actress, but as a movie columnist was most known for her outrageously decorated hats which she wore with pride at every function whether it was a casual or a dressy affair. For those who knew both women, all agreed that at times they were more

Giving out hundreds of presents to kids in the audience of the Warner Bros. Theatre on Hollywood Blvd. An annual event for me. © Turner Entertainment Co., A Warner Bros. Entertainment Inc. Company. All Rights Reserved.

colorful than the people that they wrote about and therefore stories would circulate like wildfire around the bars and living rooms of the Hollywood "In" crowd.

We used to hear people talk about the truckloads of presents that used to be delivered at Louella Parsons' home at Christmas time. The senders of these gifts were studio heads and actors on every level of success and after all the packages had been unloaded, Parsons' secretaries would carefully list the names of the gift givers along with a detailed description of each gift. This list would then be carefully filed away until the time arrived when a studio was about to release an especially expensive and prestigious movie and an actor had acquired a much sought-after part. The list would be brought out, carefully perused and then based upon the generosity of the gift given at Christmas time, the Parsons column would reflect the bounty or lack of it in the review. Needless to say, rue the mogul who inadvertently forgot to send one at all!

Nowadays most of the entertainment gossip comes from television

At MGM for Freddie Bartholemew's birthday party. Back: Bonita Granville and Judy Garland. Front: me and Tommy Kelly. In the back partially in the dark, Dickie Moore.

programs like *Entertainment Tonight* and rag trades like *The Enquirer* and *The Star*, but fortunately no one person wields the power of a Parsons or a Hopper. In a minor way, there may be one exception. For the past number of years, a few men have been making a nice living providing producers with stars to attend functions to salt the turnout of a benefit show or to provide them to appear on documentaries on programs such as *Biography*. For some imagined slight or simply because they do not personally care for the star, these men eliminate all but their favorite celebrities to these organizations, and it is a tragic situation for the stars who still have hopes of strengthening their lagging careers through some needed public exposure. It's a petty situation, propagated by petty people, not unusual in the political clime of Hollywood.

Like most of the public, I am fascinated when stars of the past are interviewed on television but I find myself disagreeing with them when they say that the studio contract system was tantamount to slavery. I suppose on the subject of money if one compares the astronomical salaries that the stars get today with the ones of the past, it very well might seem inequitable until you realize that the economy was quite different then. A

"Bonding" with Mike Curtiz on the set of *Little Big Shot*. The gentlemen in the back wearing white slacks and dark blazers were part of the Reception Committee in sales.
© Turner Entertainment Co., A Warner Bros. Entertainment Inc. Company.
All Rights Reserved.

dollar went a lot further and, considering that in 1934 a bus driver could comfortably support his family on an annual salary of $1,373.00, just imagine what fifty times that amount could do.

Hollywood has always been a mecca for young people seeking a movie career, but sadly nowadays the odds of getting a break are quite dismal. Consider the membership of the Screen Actors Guild. Nationwide there are some 95,000 registered actors but only a minuscule number will get work on a regular basis. Of course, I am not implying that everyone who came to Hollywood in the old days was guaranteed a big break, but the very fact that the studios made it a fairly regular policy to interview new-

Warners corporate CEOs visiting their new child star, with director Michael Curtiz on the set of *Little Big Shot*, 1935. © Turner Entertainment Co., A Warner Bros. Entertainment Inc. Company. All Rights Reserved.

comers and sign some of them to a limited contract made the odds very much better than today.

I have deliberately taken the time in the beginning of this chapter to acquaint you with the clime of Hollywood at that time because it has a direct bearing on why there was a mad dash for the studios to find their own child star. We were barely coming out of the Depression era and the studio heads were wise enough to look into the past and see that the innocence of a child helped to water down the harsher facts of life experienced generally by the American public.

Child stars have always been popular and contrary to the belief that the kiddie era started in the 1930s, one only has to go back to the silent era, where Mary Pickford won the hearts of the public. Little Mary, as she was called, couldn't legitimately be labeled a child movie star because although she began her career on the stage at the age of five, she didn't act in movies until she was sixteen years old. Incredibly, she came across with such childlike innocence with her sad and expressive eyes and cascading

Me as Becky, Shirley Temple as Sara and Mary Nash as Miss Minchin
in *The Little Princess*.

blond curls, she was accepted in childlike roles until she was well into her
thirties!

In that same silent era there was a most popular boy star by the name
of Jackie Coogan, who practically stole the movie *The Kid* away from his
comic genius co-star, Charlie Chaplin. In the sound era which was just
around the corner, Jackie Cooper broke the public's heart as the little boy
who idolized his over-the-hill boxer-father portrayed by Wallace Beery.
Usually remakes are not as good as the original but many years later Jon
Voight and Ricky Schroeder did a very fine job in the exceptionally good
movie, *The Champ*.

There were also two very talented British boys who came to this
country and gained fine reputations for themselves. One was Freddie
Bartholomew, who was unforgettable in the title role of *David Copperfield*,
and as the spoiled brat who becomes humanized by a fisherman played by
Spencer Tracy in MGM's *Captains Courageous*. I think because Freddie
and I both had English accents, we were supposed to do a record album of
Shakespearian plays for the Decca label, and we had even started rehears-

Jackie Coogan and myself as co-emcees at a kids award show. He was a major kid star, but the "now" kids would know him from TV as Uncle Fester.

My very first Warner Bros. movie, *Little Big Shot*. © Turner Entertainment Co., A Warner Bros. Entertainment Inc. Company. All Rights Reserved.

ing "Romeo and Juliet," but fortunately it never came to fruition. I never felt comfortable with it and I don't think Freddie did either. I did attend some of his birthday parties, but regrettably we never got the opportunity to work together again. Sadly, Freddie is no longer with us.

The other English boy was the multi-talented Roddy McDowall. Like all of his contemporaries, I adored Roddy, but I also admired him very much because, as fine an actor that he was, the adult Roddy never settled for just an acting career. He was a fine photographer with many photographic books to his credit, became a director, a producer, a musical stage and radio star, and did them all to perfection. My grandson's favorite character in *Planet of the Apes* was Roddy's and when Roddy phoned me just two days before he died, Daniel answered the phone and was thrilled to talk to him, but for that brief moment.

Of course, the epitome of the child star was neatly wrapped up into one cute talented bundle called Shirley Temple. She handily led the parade of junior stars by quite a stretch, but, even so, individually, the rest of us kids had quite a following of our own. One of the main reasons that Jack Warner brought me over from London to become his studio's first child star under a long-term contract was to give Twentieth Century Fox's box office champ a little bit of competition and in the interim make money for himself and his studio. To a degree, both goals were realized until a number of years later when he and all of the rest of the movie moguls saw the writing on the wall that the child star era was coming to a close.

One of the main reasons for this was because all of us were no longer cute and talented babies but were now turning into budding pre-teenagers. Pre-teens are neither fish nor fowl and coupled with the public's reluctance to let us grow up, it showed up in the only way that counted in Hollywood and that was in the sharp decline in the ticket sales to our movies. It was now very much the Garland-Rooney era.

In looks, Shirley Temple and I were complete opposites. She was the ideal image of a child, with a peaches-and-cream complexion that was enhanced with incredible dimples and topped off by the never-to-be-forgotten golden Temple curls. My image was that of a child with eerily mature looks that peeped out of a baby face with expressive big blue eyes and black hair styled in a Dutch bob. I always found it a strange experience when I went out in public and saw little girls who had either a head full of tightly wound curls or a very straight bob with bangs. Admittedly, the curls outnumbered the bobs by two to one.

As I look back over the years, I find it almost incredulous that I never saw a Shirley Temple movie until the premiere of *The Little Princess* in which she starred and I had a prominent part. Of course, I had seen Shirley's picture on the covers of movie magazines, but I had never met her, much less seen her movies. There was a reason for this. One of Jack Warner's dictums was that I was never to see a Temple movie because he wanted me to retain my uniqueness and not copy any of the golden child's mannerisms. I find this very odd considering the storylines that I was given in many of my Warner movies. In the studio's attempt to bend over backwards to make me as different from Shirley as they could, I'll let you judge for yourself if they succeeded. It matters not which movie came first because the end result was the same.

Shirley made *Little Miss Marker* and I did its clone *Little Big Shot*. In *Wee Willie Winkie*, Shirley visited her army grandfather in India and when trouble arose she was responsible for arranging the peace between the warring sides. In my two-reel Technicolor short, *The Littlest Diplomat*, I visit my grandfather in the army in India and when I am kidnapped by the

I'm a granddaughter of a British Colonel, captured by the enemy in Afghanistan, in the Technicolor short, *The Little Diplomat*, 1936. © Turner Entertainment Co., A Warner Bros. Entertainment Inc. Company. All Rights Reserved.

An off-the-set publicity shot of Ruby Keeler, Hugh Herbert and myself during *A Day at Santa Anita*. © Turner Entertainment Co., A Warner Bros. Entertainment Inc. Company. All Rights Reserved.

Director Michael Curtiz gives me some directions for an upcoming dramatic scene in *Little Big Shot*. © Turner Entertainment Co., A Warner Bros. Entertainment Inc. Company. All Rights Reserved.

Khan's men and taken to him in his tent, I convince him that what he was doing was wrong and therefore prevent a war between Afghanistan and the British Empire. In *Susanna of the Mounties*, Shirley is the only survivor of an Indian massacre, but is ultimately responsible for improved relations between the Indians and the Canadians. In my two-reel Technicolor short, *The Little Pioneer*, I am the only survivor of an African massacre, but stop further bloodshed by preventing more warfare between the African natives and the South African Boers and the British. Going one step further, in the case of *Captain January* and my *Captain's Kid*, Shirley and I even shared the same co-star, the irrepressible and lovable Guy Kibbee.

Woman Doctor, 1938. As his daughter, it was my first time working with friend, Henry Wilcoxen, and my second time with Claire Dodd and Frieda Inescourt (not shown) in this movie.

Me and good pal Roddy McDowall at the Jeanette MacDonald Club. Everyone loved
Roddy and we sorely miss his presence. © Turner Entertainment Co., A Warner
Bros. Entertainment Inc. Company. All Rights Reserved.

The next comparison is a bit of a stretch but nevertheless still a con-
nection. In 1936, I made another two-reel Technicolor short called *A Day
at Santa Anita*, and in 1949 David O. Selznick lent Shirley to Warners for
a movie called *The Story of Seabiscuit*.

An interesting sidelight to my *A Day at Santa Anita* is that my guest
stars in cameo appearances were Al Jolson, Ruby Keeler, Bette Davis, Edward G. Robinson and Olivia de Havilland, to name a few. In the uncut
version of the short, there were two other guest stars, but Jack Warner
made sure they were edited out. He had lost interest in them and refused
to give them further exposure in one of his productions. The lady was
Virginia Bruce and the man was...Clark Gable!

My years with Warners had been productive and established my name
in the movie world so much so that when my contract was up at Warner
Bros., two weeks had not elapsed before I was signed to do a movie at
Republic Studios called *Woman Doctor*. It was far from a Sybil Jason starrer
and at a studio essentially known for producing "B" westerns, but it was a
movie based on a very popular novel of the day and the producer was
going to be Sol Siegel, who would eventually move to Twentieth Century-Fox to produce some of the popular Marilyn Monroe movies.

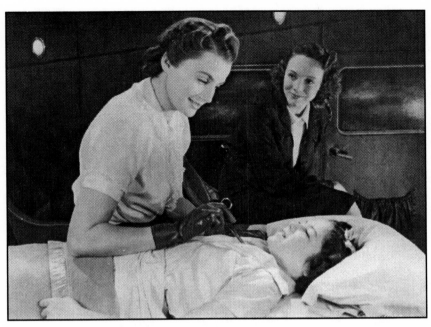

Woman Doctor, 1938. Frieda Inescourt as my mother "saving my life" and femme fatale Claire Dodd looking on.

This scene in *The Little Princess* gave me the willies. They gave me a real chicken to pluck and I absolutely hated it! As an adult I always made sure that any chicken that I got was already plucked! © Turner Entertainment Co., A Warner Bros. Entertainment Inc. Company. All Rights Reserved.

The last scene in *The Bluebird*. This is a joyous scene, but I personally was scared stiff of the bird. It kept on struggling to fly out of my hands. When it finally did, on cue, I was one relieved little actress! © 20th Century-Fox Pictures. All Rights Reserved.

The leads were all prominent actors from other studios and to my delight I learned that I would be reunited with two ladies I had worked with at Warner Bros. Playing my mother once again was Frieda Inescourt, who had done the same in *The Great O'Malley*, and Claire Dodd, repeating her characterization as the "other woman," as she had in *The Singing Kid*. In the role of my father would be Henry Wilcoxon, who was well known for his portrayal of Antony to Claudette Colbert's Cleopatra long before the advent of the spectacular production that starred Elizabeth Taylor and Richard Burton. As an actor, Henry had had a successful and active career, but in his later years he held the prestigious position as personal assistant to Cecil B. DeMille at Paramount Studios. Making *Woman Doctor* was a very

The Bluebird, 1940. I play Angela Berlingot, the little crippled girl, looking sadly after Myltyl (Shirley) who has just refused to trade the bird that she captured in the woods for Angela's only real possession, her doll. © 20th Century-Fox Pictures. All Rights Reserved.

A rare picture of me and Shirley in a scene from *The Bluebird*. She is pictured inside my house soon after I discover I can walk. All of this was cut from the movie!
© 20th Century-Fox Pictures. All Rights Reserved.

A short but scary moment on Sea Biscuit's back for a publicity shot while filming *A Day at Santa Anita*. © Turner Entertainment Co., A Warner Bros. Entertainment Inc. Company. All Rights Reserved.

pleasant experience for me as I became very close to Henry and Claire Dodd. At every lunch time Anita and I would make a foursome with the two of them and walk from the studio lot across Ventura Boulevard to a restaurant to eat and to relax before going back to work for the rest of the day.

Even after the movie had been completed, friendship with Henry and his beautiful actress-wife Joan Woodbury, would continue on. One of my fondest memories was spending weekends at their beautiful ranch and being allowed to stay up late to listen to the radio show *Inner Sanctum*.

Halfway through the filming of *Woman Doctor*, two contract offers came through for me. One was from MGM and the other one was from Twentieth Century-Fox. Why my agent chose Fox, I will never know, but I would guess it was because they offered more money. Of course, Anita and I were very excited that once more I would be associated with a major studio, but it wasn't long before we moved onto the Fox lot that stark reality set in. We should have recognized a warning signal with our first meeting with Darryl F. Zanuck to sign the actual contract. The meeting

Anita, my uncle Harry and I at an exhibitor's luncheon honoring those of us that did well at the box office. © Turner Entertainment Co., A Warner Bros. Entertainment Inc. Company. All Rights Reserved.

took place in his office and his attitude toward us was frigid. He barely acknowledged my presence and the conversation with Anita mainly centered on my salary. In essence, he was reneging on the amount agreed upon by my agent and the studio and in its stead offered an insulting amount. Anita reminded him of the original agreement and, when he remained adamant on his offer, Anita politely told him that it would not be acceptable and, hand in hand, we headed for the door.

Zanuck stopped us, saying he would agree to the original terms and requested that I sign the contract then and there. My sister Anita was a very down-to-earth type of person and I don't believe that she was ever under the illusion that I was going to get the same kind of treatment that I had at Warners, yet, on the other hand, I'm sure she didn't ever envision what came to be a most heartbreaking experience.

Now that I was officially a Fox contract player, it seemed to take forever before I was assigned to a movie so for the first time in my life, my sister decided to send me to a public school. She felt that being in contact with

A scene from *The Little Princess* with Cesar Romero and Shirley Temple. © Turner Entertainment Co., A Warner Bros. Entertainment Inc. Company. All Rights Reserved.

regular kids would be a good experience for me, as well as a good opportunity to help me lose what remained of my English accent. Rightly so, she felt that my acting opportunities would be enhanced if I became more Americanized but, despite all good intentions, my experience at the Beverly Hills school was not a happy one. With very few exceptions the kids really made it rough for "little miss movie star" and the teachers themselves were in the untenable situation where they dare not give me too much attention as a student in case that would be taken for preferential treatment.

I was most relieved when my first movie assignment for Fox came through and that I now would be going to school on the studio lot. I was ecstatic when we found out the movie was based on the classic story by Francis Hodgson Burnett, *The Little Princess*, and that I was going to work with Shirley Temple! She was to star as Sara Crewe, the little rich girl whose father reluctantly places her in Miss Minchin's School for Girls when he goes off to war, and I was cast as the little maid, Becky, whom she befriends. Initially, it was a disappointment to see how skimpy my part was but eventually as shooting progressed my part was greatly enlarged.

The Little Pioneer, a 1938 color short. Note the older lady who two years later played Shirley Temple's deceased grandmother in *Bluebird*. © Turner Entertainment Co., A Warner Bros. Entertainment Inc. Company. All Rights Reserved.

One day before our first day of shooting, it occurred to my sister that in the classic story the little maid Becky was a cockney. No one at the studio had ever mentioned anything about an accent for me but just to be on the safe side Anita phoned the studio and made the enquiry. A sense of panic prevailed because we were within hours of our first day shoot and the studio had wrongly assumed that because I was English I could do the cockney accent. First of all, I had never heard a cockney accent in my life and by this time I had lived and worked in America for almost six years. Keeping a cool head, and knowing that I had always had a talent for mimicry, Anita suggested that if the studio could run a movie for me where the accent was used she felt that there was a good chance that I might be able to pick up on it.

They told us to come to the studio immediately and when we got there, they hurried us to a projection room. There I saw *Pygmalion*, the original nonmusical *My Fair Lady*, which starred the marvelous British actress, Wendy Hiller. That evening at home, Anita and I worked diligently on the accent and

The Technicolor short, *The Little Pioneer*, 1938. Left to right: Jane Wyman, me and Tommy Cook. Ronald Reagan at the time was courting Jane early in their relationship. © Turner Entertainment Co., A Warner Bros. Entertainment Inc. Company. All Rights Reserved.

much to our and the studio's relief, I came in the next morning with a cockney accent. Many years later I wrote a letter to Dame Wendy Hiller in London and related this story to her. I thanked her for being partially responsible for me winning the New York Film Critics/*Hollywood Reporter* award for Best Supporting Actress of 1939. In response, I received a lovely letter from her explaining how she researched her cockney accent for *Pygmalion* and she graciously included an autographed picture of herself to me.

As an adult I am always amazed when reporters and authors of books all try to get me to say something derogatory about Shirley Temple. Of course, none of them have succeeded for the simple fact there is absolutely nothing derogatory that I could say about her. She had been a joy to work with and although no one could have described us as bosom buddies when we were children, we really did have a good working relationship.

As much as I would have liked it, it was difficult to get close to Shirley because Mrs. Temple was extremely protective of her and inevitably when our scenes together had been completed, Shirley would be escorted back to her trailer dressing room. However, I did enjoy the few times we sat outside of her trailer and designed clothes for our paper dolls. The incongruity of this is that every child in America must have owned a Shirley Temple paper doll and a fair amount had Sybil Jason paper dolls, but neither of us used either one ourselves. We preferred to design our own dolls!

Sometimes we would get very arty and Shirley would draw pictures of her Pekinese dogs and I would draw tropical island scenes. At times like these we were no different than any other little girls in America.

However, as compatible as we were, there was a vast difference in the treatment that was accorded us on the set as well as off of it. As Fox's top moneymaker it is not hard to understand that Shirley would have all of the accoutrements that befitted her star status but that didn't make it any easier for me, who not too long ago had the same kind of treatment at Warners. I had no dressing room of any kind as I was asked to come to the set fully dressed in my costume as Becky, and a small section of the soundstage was delegated as my schoolroom and doubled as my place to relax in between scenes. Shirley and I were just kids in circumstances like these and these types of decisions were not made by her or me. These were strictly the bailiwick of the adults and the studio VIP's!

I must preface this next story by saying Anita and I knew the director Walter Lang on a social level and spent many a nice Sunday at his and his wife's beautiful home in Beverly Hills. His wife was known to all their friends as "Fieldsie" and, just like her best friend Carole Lombard, she was a fun person to know. As a matter of fact, when Miss Lombard died tragically in a plane crash, she had willed many of her treasures to Fieldsie. For me, it was the best set of circumstances that Walter was our director on *The Little Princess* and *The Bluebird*. Walter and his wife had a lovely sensitive nature, but they also had outrageous senses of humor which is very well illustrated in this next story and, knowing them as well as I did, I found it just as hilarious as everyone else did.

In the movie, Shirley's character was named Sara and mine was Becky and in this particular scene, through a set of circumstances, Sara is now delegated to the same attic rooms as Becky. One night Sara wakes up to discover that her room has been transformed into a cozy warm place with a lit fireplace and a supply of satin blankets, robes and slippers, and a table-full of hot and enticing food. She calls out to Becky who is in her own attic room and although the little scullery maid is amazed by the transformation of Sara's room, always being very hungry she is particularly mesmerized by the food. Walter wanted to illustrate this and ordered me to stuff my mouth full of muffins when Shirley and I sat down at the table.

I was having a really tough time saying my lines clearly while still retaining the cockney accent. It didn't help one bit that after we filmed the first take, Walter said there was a problem with the sound and that we'd have to do a repeat take. We did and I stuffed my mouth once again. But at the end of this take, Walter apologized profusely and said the lighting was casting a shadow on both Shirley's and my faces. By this time, I felt like my face was turning green from all the muffins I ingested—but a third take was ordered and we started in once again. This scene was a few seconds shorter in the finished version of the movie, but take note the next time you see the attic scene. You will see the beginning of an uncontrolled giggle from Shirley while she watched me trying to talk with a mouthful of muffins. When Walter yelled "CUT," she really let go with a laugh!

Lunchtime was called and, although I couldn't look at food, Anita and I still headed for the Fox commissary, the Café de Paris, and when we reached our regular table and saw what was on it, we looked at each other and burst out laughing. Smack dab in the middle of the table was the largest bowl of muffins you ever did see and we knew then that our friend and director had been up to his old tricks with all the retakes and the proliferation of muffins!

The Little Princess, as far as an acting job went, was a marvelous experience for me. Even though the character of Becky was a big departure for me, I realized how very much I enjoyed doing character work and when the movie was released and the reviews came out, the picture was a big success and my personal reviews were beyond our wildest expectations.

In fact, rarely did Louella Parsons and Hedda Hopper agree on anything but they both applauded my work as Becky and both wrote the same comment: "Let's have more of Sybil Jason." In the March 4, 1939 issue of the widely-read *The Hollywood Spectator,* the reviewer wrote, "If there be any adult player on the screen who can give a finer, more understanding, more poignant performance than little Sybil Jason contributes to this picture, I herewith nominate him or her for next year's Academy acting award without waiting to see the performance." I would say this is pretty heavy stuff and apparently this same gentleman had reviewed a 1936 movie of mine and referred to it in this manner. "If any producer had shared my opinion then, Sybil today would be one of our big box office stars. That is what her appearance in *The Little Princess* will do for her now but why the delay?"

My agent was floating on air and predicted that in his opinion I would be one of the few kid stars to overcome the so-called curse and instead segue into a successful adult career.

Of course, Anita and I felt very uplifted, but that didn't last long for it seemed ever since I had signed a contract with Fox there appeared to be a fly in the ointment. It came in the form of a rumor that turned up in several gossip columns and in essence said that because I had received such good reviews in *The Little Princess*, and had won awards for my work in it, Mrs. Temple would never allow me to work with Shirley again.

The first Warner Bros. publicity still of me they sent out to the public. © Turner Entertainment Co., A Warner Bros. Entertainment Inc. Company. All Rights Reserved.

Unfortunately the rumor spread, gained momentum, and this put Anita and I on edge. The silence from the studio was deafening. There were no pats on the back for a job well done, no hints for a follow-up movie…nothing!

It was with a sheer sense of relief that the studio finally informed us that I was going to be in Shirley's next movie, and the swiftness of the publicity department getting this information out to all of the major newspapers and magazines in town made our heads spin!

The movie was going to be a version of Maurice Maeterlinck's classic tale of *The Blue Bird*, and the studio stated that this movie would have an unprecedented big budget, unlike anything issued to their productions in the past.

Usually when one received a finalized script of a movie, you are apprised of the shooting date. We were quite puzzled when a good two weeks before that date I was told to report to the studio early one morning. When we arrived, we were directed to go to a specific soundstage, and when we got inside all we saw was a small lit set with a plain backdrop and two chairs facing each other.

One of the chairs faced the camera and the other one was placed behind it. I was greeted and handed a few pages from the *Blue Bird* script. It contained only Shirley's lines and those of the various characters that would appear in the movie. It didn't take a rocket scientist to figure out that this was going to be the ultimate humiliation for me. I was expected to read Shirley's lines so that actors could screen test for the various roles like the Father, the character Light and the "deceased" grandparents. As young as I was, I knew I wasn't being treated right and I could see from the hurt look in my sister's eyes that she too felt that way but, considering the position I was now placed in, there wasn't much we could do about it.

After a couple of days of reading for the tests, I could now concentrate and prepare for my role as Angela Berlingot, the little crippled girl who yearns for the bird that Mytyl (Shirley) and Tytyl (Johnny Russell) had captured in the woods.

My part in *The Blue Bird* was, to put it politely, minuscule. It consisted of a scene in the beginning of the movie and another at the end. Although it didn't afford me much screen time, we did count on my being remembered for a dramatic moment near the end of the movie. When Mytyl stops being a selfish little girl and discovers the true meaning of happiness, she decides to bring what she thinks is the Bluebird of Happiness to the cripple Angela and through this unselfish act a miracle takes place. Angela discovers that she can walk and after a few faltering steps both girls walk out of the front door where the cripple girl's mother is amazed that her child can walk and runs off excitedly to tell her husband the good news. When Mytyl hands the bluebird over to Angela, it escapes the little girl's hand and she bursts into tears at her loss. The movie ends with a close-up of Mytyl explaining that nothing is lost because true happiness can always be discovered in your own front yard.

After the movie was completed, we got the usual silent treatment from the studio but as our experience had told us it wouldn't be too long before they informed us when to turn up for the preview and then hopefully news of my next assignment.

One week before the preview of the movie, instead of getting a call from the studio telling us what time to arrive at the theatre, we got one from Walter Lang asking us if we would be good enough to come to his office at the studio. This was our friend, so we really didn't have too many misgivings, although Anita still felt a bit skittish as she did with anything out of the ordinary that happened to be connected to the studio. The word 'uneasy' turned out to be the understatement of the year. After our initial pleasantries with Walter, he seemed to look visibly uncomfortable and hem and hawed for quite a while. He finally got to the point of the meeting. He prefaced the bombshell by assuring us that the scene where Angela discovers that she can walk was probably the finest one in the whole movie—but he had to edit it out. He explained that his hands had been tied because Mrs. Temple told Mr. Zanuck if that scene stayed in, she and Shirley would walk out of the studio. In a business sense I can see that if push came to shove, the studio would do anything to please the guardians of their top box office star, but there was never any doubt that Mr. Zanuck always considered me an inconvenience and did not find it hard to treat me accordingly. I was not the first person he would do this to, nor would I be the las,t but because Anita and I decided that we didn't need any further humiliation we did not attend the preview.

When the reviews came out on *The Blue Bird*, they were not very good. Besides lambasting the movie, many of the columnists and reviewers picked up on the puzzling abruptness of the classic story in the last scene where the crippled girl is seen standing up on her own with no explanation of how that was accomplished.

As I now peruse a couple of my pressbooks, I see that several reviewers considered *The Blue Bird* a bomb and quite inferior to the popular *The Wizard of Oz*. I cannot agree with that rather cruel comparison. *The Blue Bird* was a beautifully photographed movie, and I believe the fire sequence in the forest was second to none and deservedly earned an Academy Award for the special effects man, Fred Sersen.

In the ensuing weeks after the release of the movie, my time was spent doing guest shots on radio, appearing at charity affairs, and attending my contemporaries' birthday parties. The weeks turned into months and although I was not dropped from the studio, neither was I put to work; there was no word from the studio one way or the other. Finally it was decided that I should go on a worldwide personal appearance tour which would get me some much-needed attention and gain back some of my popularity. Realistically, a good movie part would have done the same thing for me but that was not forthcoming because Fox was not cooperating in advancing my career. Instead they used, as bait, the news that the last country on our itinerary was going to be South Africa and they would even pay me for a six-week non-working vacation until it was time to return to America. Our hands were tied but at least it would give me something to do and we'd have the wonderful experience of seeing our family again.

All things considered, the tour turned out to be an incredible experience for a twelve-year-old child for it was a geographical plethora of sights and sounds and cultures that were presented under the most ideal conditions.

By ship, Anita and I left the port of San Pedro and continued on to San Francisco. Although I did not have an appearance date there, we did spend a lovely two days visiting with some friends and taking in a few shows. After that, our long journey started, beginning with Hawaii where I appeared on radio and talked about *The Blue Bird*, and our pending visits to the Orient and finally to South Africa. Travel was not new to me but traveling to countries I had only read about was mind-boggling. We toured China, Japan, India, Singapore, Manila, and in each country I was treated like royalty by both the public and the press. One must remember that unlike today, seeing movie stars in their own country was a very unusual sight and therefore my presence caused quite a bit of a stir especially in China and Japan. Our newspapermen/escorts explained to Anita and I that my movies had always been popular in the Orient and a lot of it had to do with my being small of stature and the way I wore my hair. For once there wasn't a curl in sight and everywhere I looked were kids that looked just like me. Well, almost.

Visiting the Orient was very exciting, but also very horrific! The first sight that greeted our eyes when we came into Hong Kong was a dead body floating down the river. As awful a sight as that was, each morning when we left our hotel to go to a theater to make an appearance, we saw dead bodies all piled up against each other in the doorways of office buildings where they went at night to get shelter against the cold. It was not unusual to see a dead body laying in the street and when we asked our escort why nobody saw to their removal, the man told us that it was understood that anyone who touched a dead body would then be responsible for its burial.

This was a real eye opener for me and I think, with this glimpse into a very harsh reality, a significant part of my childhood disappeared. To my sorrow, I saw a repeat of this human suffering in the next few countries that were left on our itinerary, and with a sense of relief and excitement our ship headed for South Africa.

America had not entered the war as yet but Great Britain and all of its dominions had, so when our ship finally docked in Cape Town it was not very hard to spot our parents because they were the only two people allowed on the dock due to strict wartime restrictions. They had to get special clearance to greet us, but because of all the publicity that preceded our arrival and my being a public personage, a lot of red tape had been eliminated and cleared for our reunion.

There were some awkward moments when we greeted each other because our parents had had an unfriendly divorce a number of years before and so my sister and I had to take turns embracing them. When I was with my mother, Anita was with my father, and then we'd switch. It was not exactly an ideal situation for any of us but, considering everything, we all seemed to handle it quite well.

As soon as our papers had cleared and our luggage released, we said goodbye to our father and promised him that we'd get together with him the very next day. We then left with our mother to go to her home where we would be living during our stay in South Africa.

I don't think it showed, but I was a bundle of nerves when we stepped through the front door and saw wall-to-wall relatives waiting to greet us. How utterly strange it was to be introduced to my own brother, my eldest sister, aunts and uncles and cousins by the dozens. They were all very welcoming and warm, but at the same time I felt like I was something being examined under a microscope. I was their flesh and blood yet quite alien to them and their society. Thankfully, I could take refuge in one familiar face of someone I had always loved and had never forgotten.

It was the face of my stepfather. For years, he had been an executive with African Theatres, Ltd., where he had started out as a theatre manager. He was an accomplished musician and had conducted the Cape Town Civic Orchestra when I was just a tot starting out on my career. Everyone in Cape Town knew and loved my "Uncle Mickey" and because he was now my stepfather it didn't take us long to pick up where we had left off in a very loving relationship.

The next two days were filled to capacity with activity. We had to cram a lot in because on the third day, just as Anita and I started to bond with our family, we had to leave on the South African tour. The only thing that made this palatable was the thought that when the tour was over we would have a whole six weeks to spend together before Anita and I were scheduled to return to America.

The tour went beautifully and everywhere I went I played to capacity audiences. It was not unlike my American tours in that, besides appearing on the various stages of the theatres from Cape Town to Johannesburg and everything in between, I also visited orphanages, hospitals, schools and met many dignitaries at various social functions. One of my most memorable meetings was with General Jan Smuts who became Premiere of South Africa. He presented me with a beautiful badge that was only given out to born South Africans who had brought honor upon their country.

One evening in Cape Town one of my movies was playing at the Alhambra Theater and Mrs. Smuts attended the special showing. I was quite short for a twelve-year-old, yet even at that I was at least a half a head taller than Mrs. Smuts who was very petite and wore her salt-and-pepper-colored hair in short and tightly wound curls. She was quite the pixie and while the photographers were taking our picture in the theater lobby she squeezed my arm and with twinkling eyes informed me "You know MY name is Sybil too!"

It was when we were in Johannesburg on the last lap of our tour that everything that I had known in the past exciting and glamorous seven years just collapsed around me. We received the devastating news that

Pearl Harbor had been attacked and although I was now in the country of my birth, I had lived in America long enough to consider that my real home. Naturally, my family wouldn't hear of Anita and I returning to Hollywood now that America was in the war so for the remainder of World War II, I remained in South Africa.

I shall not go extensively into that period of my life because it would digress from this book, which is essentially about my career, but I would like to mention a few things that readers might find of interest.

Needless to say, I was very homesick for California but what helped me considerably was being named the mascot of the USO in Cape Town. One of my duties was to make all the boys feel welcome and to ask them if there was anything special we could do for them. Without exception they asked if I would write to their parents, wife or girlfriend and assure them that they were okay, but missing them very much. I wrote a steady flow of these letters and even managed to stay in touch with some of them up until the very end of the war.

One of my very favorite times at the USO was listening to the Armed Forces Radio shows. Bob Hope was a fairly regular guest, but I would get a pang of loneliness when I heard the voices of some of my friends like Lana Turner and Judy Garland. It was a reminder how far away I was from America and my career.

Although I spent a lot of time at the USO, I did not neglect our own South African boys in the Service. My mother, my two sisters and I were excellent knitters and we could always be found fashioning gloves, socks and scarves for the boys. The government would supply the kahki wool and we would supply the work.

Unfortunately, there were times when the horror of war was brought home to me and my family. My mother's home was just a short walk to the beach and sometimes when I took my morning constitutional I would see oil slick and debris floating in our ocean.

More personally, my heart broke when I heard that my favorite cousin had been killed in the war. He was a very handsome young man, very much like Errol Flynn, and was a pilot in the South African Air Force. He lost his life when he bailed out of his downed plane in Tobruk and while dangling from his parachute was riddled with bullets by enemy fire.

I have been so fortunate in my lifetime to have traveled so extensively around the world and when I am asked about South Africa, I can honestly say that it is probably one of the most beautiful countries I have ever seen or lived in. It took an American gentleman to so aptly describe its beauty by telling me this most charming tale. He said that when God was creating the world, He held a basket full of jewels in His hand and into each country He would drop a beautiful gem. However, when He got to Cape Town...He tripped!

My family was never under the delusion that after the war I would settle down in Cape Town, so it came as no surprise that when peace was declared I immediately put in my request for a quota number in order to be able to return to America. The immigration laws were very strict at that time and only a limited amount of quota numbers was being issued to each country every year. The waiting list was very long and in some cases it took as many as five years to obtain one. There was also the problem of transportation. Ships and planes out of South Africa to America were not on a regular scheduled basis right after the war and if one was lucky enough to get a quota number it was a miracle if one could get booked onto a ship.

Fortunately for me, both came through at the same time and I was scheduled to leave the country on May 7, 1946. I was both ecstatic and scared to death, for I was returning to America alone because by now Anita was happily married and had settled down permanently in Cape Town.

On the night before my departure, my dad threw me a huge going-away dinner party that was held in one of the city's finest hotels. We had no sooner been seated at our various tables when the hotel manager approached our head table and whispered something into my dad's ear. My father looked visibly shaken and got up to go where Anita was seated. He, in turn, told her something that made her turn ashen and she immediately came over to get me. I couldn't understand why they were leading me out of the restaurant, but I knew it had to be something serious.

Although we weren't staying at the hotel, the manager escorted us to a suite, asked if he could do anything for us, and then left us alone. After a long silence, my father and Anita broke the news to me that my stepfather had just been murdered. My mind went blank with shock and even though I wanted to yell and scream with sorrow, absolutely nothing came out. The party was called off and Anita and I left to go to my mother who was in a state of collapse. The next day, I cancelled my trip to America.

I never regretted the additional months that I stayed with my mother because I too was devastated by my darling "Uncle Mickey's" death. I had adored him, and he and my mother and had had such an ideal marriage. I had grown very close and protective of my mother in those months, so when the time came in November when my quota number was going to expire, I didn't know what to do. We had a family conference and with assurances coming from Anita and the family, and most importantly my mother, I was told she would be well-taken care of and that I was now to follow through with my plans. I started making inquiries as to the next ship to leave for America and to my absolute horror discovered there were no bookings available then nor in the near future. I started to panic because I had but twelve more days left and then my quota number would expire. I even called the American consulate and begged them to give me an extension but, even though they were very courteous, they said there was nothing they could do. If they bent the rules for me, they would have to do it for others.

Just when it looked like I was in a hopeless situation, we heard of six other people who were in the same boat as myself and by making some inquiries I was able to contact them. We arranged to meet and the outcome of that meeting proved to be the answer to our mutual problem. The seven of us agreed to charter a plane and although this was going to be horrendously expensive, we had no other alternative. Within that week I took the train to Johannesburg and the seven of us boarded our plane. We were finally on our way to America.

I had envisioned this scene so many times in Africa, but now I practically had to pinch myself to realize I was no longer dreaming but actually walking down Beverly Drive in Beverly Hills. As I looked around the street, I saw that physically nothing had drastically changed since I had left in 1941, but then I glanced at my reflection in a store window and realized that I was the one who had changed. I was no longer a little girl but a young lady in her late teens with all the responsibilities and concerns of an adult and although I missed my family and especially Anita very much, I was looking forward to starting a new life and perhaps the rejuvenation of a movie career. My thoughts were interrupted by the notion that I was seeing a familiar face, and as I approached the gentleman a little closer I was now sure that I did know him, but wondered if he would remember me after all this time. I had remembered him as a very dear, warm man and one I had always been fond of, but my concern was soon put to rest as soon as I told him who I was. George Temple, Shirley's dad, gave me a broad grin and a big welcoming hug and wanted to know what I had been doing for the past six years. After I brought him up to date, he said that I must get in touch with Shirley, as he was sure she'd be delighted to hear from me, and quickly wrote down her home phone number. As we parted, he reminded me to keep in touch and he said that he thought it was wonderful that I was now back in America.

That evening I did call Shirley and as her father had predicted she was genuinely happy to hear from me. We had a lengthy conversation which mainly consisted of exchanging news about each other. Of course by now Shirley was a married lady, busy with her career and husband and although we talked enthusiastically of getting together very soon, somehow or other that didn't happen for a number of years.

That Christmas, Shirley sent me a lovely holiday card and enclosed some great snapshots of her and her husband, Johnny Agar, and had inscribed each one with warm wishes from them both for the new year. They had made such a beautiful looking couple, but sadly their marriage did not last. John had a number of problems that he had to work out for himself, which he did years later, and both he and Shirley ultimately met their soulmates and had perfect second marriages. However, this was still in the future and now I had to start making plans for getting on with my own life.

My first few weeks back in California were busy ones. Many of my friends gave parties to celebrate my return to America and I had even visited the Warners lot and gotten reacquainted with a lot of people I had worked with when I was a child. I also had my first few experiences appearing on television. At that time two local channels were showing most of my Warner Bros. movies and the hosts of these shows would introduce me during their commercial breaks and I would talk about my experiences making these movies.

Most important, I also returned to my original show business roots by doing some stage work. I was cast as Dorothy in the musical play version of *The Wizard of Oz*, and it was a most happy experience for me in more ways than one.

During the day most of our first week's rehearsals were devoted to blocking, scene by scene, and then in the evenings we concentrated on line readings and solving some technical production problems.

One evening I took the opportunity for a mini break when our director was busy with our production crew and as I watched from a seat in the auditorium and leisurely sipped on a coke, a young man approached me and asked if he could sit down next to me. I had never seen him before and I knew he wasn't with the company so at first I was a bit reticent in being too friendly. However, I did half-heartedly invite him to sit down. He was a very handsome young man with beautiful blue eyes and a very outgoing personality. He explained he had gotten out of the Navy after serving four years in the war on an aircraft carrier and he had just left his home in Pennsylvania and was now enjoying his first day in California. There was no doubt I was attracted to him but when I looked into those blue eyes and listened to Anthony Drake tell me all about himself, it never dawned on me that I had just met the man I would soon marry and spend the rest of my life with ... but that's exactly what happened.

The reviews for *The Wizard of Oz* were very good and gave me enough self-confidence to sign up with an agent to get my movie career back on track. I had not made a movie in six years and although that doesn't seem like a very long time, in Hollywood years it was a hundred light years away! It did not take me long after going out on a couple of interviews for movie jobs to come to the realization that this was going to be a whole different ball game for me. In the past, I had always been under contract to a major studio and there had been no need for me to audition for a part, but I was now in a different category and found myself not too far removed from the plight of a neophyte. I had no track record as an adult actress, plus I had to continually buck the specter of other ex-child stars whose adult renderings of acting were less than favorable and left a permanent bad taste in the mouths of casting agents and producers. Unfortunately, in this millennium, I see that nothing has changed in this respect. The ex-child stars of television are experiencing the same plight that we did and until some brave souls in charge of siphoning out real talent and giving them a chance to succeed, all that those young actors can do is just keep trying and hope for the best.

At this stage of my life I took a realistic look around at what some of my contemporaries were going through and it wasn't a pretty sight. Their psyche was being attacked on a regular basis yet somehow they just bobbed up with a smile on their face like a child's toy floating in a bathtub. This tenacity, as brave as it was, was not without its consequences and took its toll in the form of excess drinking, drugs and multiple marriages. As far as I could see, that was too high a price to pay for a profession that idolized youth and ultimately would reject you for lack of it.

As much as I truly loved acting, and knew deep within my heart I could excel as a dramatic character actress, I voluntarily retired from the acting profession. I was now a married lady with a home to run and like

Composers Harold Arlen and "Yip" Harburg went on three years later to
compose songs for *The Wizard of Oz*.

most young couples my husband Tony and I entertained quite extensively
and were entertained in return by other young couples.

Naturally, that included my show business friends from the past and
it was always interesting when they kept us apprised of their activities and
the latest news circulating around Hollywood. Sadly, by this time, they
were no longer considered to be in the star stratosphere and though they
did still manage to get work, it was spasmodic and becoming quite frightening because the size of their parts was diminishing by the job. My heart
went out to them and it was at times like these that I know I had made the
right decision about retiring from acting.

As enjoyable as our social life was there came a time when Tony and I felt there was an element missing in our lives and we both agreed that element was a baby. We were extremely excited when we found out that I was pregnant and with great glee we informed our families of the good news. It was heartbreaking when I suffered a miscarriage into my second month, but that did not deter us from trying once again. It happened almost immediately but this time we decided to wait a couple of months before we told anyone the good news.

I was approaching my third month of pregnancy and everything seemed to be going very well so we phoned Tony's family and sent a cablegram off to my family in South Africa. Two days later I received a cablegram from Cape Town and instead of receiving a congratulatory message I was informed that my mother had just died. On hearing this devastating news, I suffered a shock to my system which produced the physical signs of an approaching miscarriage. Tony lost no time in getting me to my doctor, who administered a shot to ward off any further complications and ordered me to bed for essentially the rest of my pregnancy.

Our beautiful little daughter arrived five and a half weeks ahead of time and had to spend her first two weeks in the hospital putting on some weight, but what a red-letter day it was when we brought our little girl home. We named her Toni after her father and gave her the middle name of Maryanna which honored my mother, Mary, and, Tony's mother, Anna. The only sad part to this joyous occasion was that my mother didn't live to get the news of the birth of her new grandchild, but my sister Anita told me a beautiful story that eased the sadness. When they received the news of my pregnancy in the cablegram that I sent, my mother was already in a coma, but Anita was determined that somehow she could get the news through to our mother. She bent down very close to my mother's ear and said "Sybil is going to have a baby." A shadow of a smile appeared on her lips and although barely perceptible, she gave Anita's hand a slight squeeze. I cherish the thought that she knew about my baby.

Long before the birth of Toni, Anita had booked passage on a ship so that she would be with me in plenty of time for the big event, but because our little one decided to come five and a half weeks ahead of time, she missed the actual birth. How wonderful it was that when Toni was only two weeks old, and now home with her parents, Anita arrived. She took it upon herself to guide our little princess into a happy and healthy babyhood, and was well on her way to spoiling all three of us in the six weeks she stayed at our home. My heart broke when her visit came to an end but within a week of her departure, my husband's mother, his stepfather, and his eldest sister, Ann, arrived and showered us with more family affection and hourly comments on the perfection of our child. Eventually all of our visitors returned to their homes and the three of us settled down to establishing our own daily routine.

We lived in Toluca Lake at that time, which is right near Warner Bros., and almost daily, my baby and I would walk over to the studio and join some of the Warner people at the studio's drugstore that was located just off the lot. Over a coke or an ice cream, I chatted regularly with a gentleman who had been an editor on most of my movies in the old days and he was always shaking his head in wonderment that baby Sybil was now a mother. There was no doubt about it—I was a full-time mom and enjoying every moment of it.

The ensuing years were busy ones for me with the upbringing of our daughter the absolute priority for Tony and I. The economy was good at that time and allowed us to supply our child with the security of a stay-at-home-mother and a father who left early for work in the morning and returned home at night to bond and to plan out fun activities for the weekend for our family's enjoyment.

As our child grew older, I became heavily involved in the PTA and taking Toni to ballet and tap lessons. In fact, I found myself "becoming Anita," in that I was making costumes for her dance recitals and wardrobe for the stage plays she was in which were held at the city's parks and recreation facilities. Although Toni had a sweet singing voice, played the piano very well, was an excellent dancer and could have become a good little actress, she only enjoyed displaying these talents as an extra-curricular activity. This was fine with my husband and myself because we never considered her a clone of ourselves, but as a separate entity who would eventually choose what she most enjoyed doing later on in life. As a result, Toni developed into a very happy and fulfilled young woman.

For the most part, my life was filled with Toni's activities until she was almost out of junior high school. I had and still have an interest in anything to do with children and I started doing quite a number of benefit appearances that aided churches, synagogues, and just about any organization that helped needy children. I was able to do this because my old movies were still playing on television and it was very nice feeling to know that because of my past work, it was now, in a roundabout way, being put to good use in helping to make life a little easier for kids who needed a foot up to get over some rough spots in their lives. However, I must admit that this was not just a one-way street. It gave me a long forgotten rush of adrenalin to appear in public once again and receive the acceptance that only an audience can give to a performer. As Toni was on the verge of starting high school, it was her time to spread her wings, develop her own friendships and interests and there was no doubt that she didn't need me as much as she had in the past. She knew that I would always be there for her, but just not residing in her back pocket anymore.

Now, without a sense of guilt, I gave in to the urge to do something creative and I was doubly fortunate to have a husband who had always backed me up in whatever I wished to do. When I told him of my urge to break out and do something creative, he got right to the point and said, "Go for it!" This was a wonderful assurance, but there was one major problem. I didn't know what to go for! After several weeks of mulling over different ideas I was still at a loss for what direction to head in until one night when Tony and I attended a political event held at the Hollywood Palladium. We had been invited because of the charity work I had been doing for the various organizations here in California, and one of the city council members had already honored me with a beautiful hand-crafted certificate at a ceremony at City Hall, and now had extended this invitation to attend this event.

Amongst our dinner companions at the table assigned to us was a gentleman by the name of William Thrush, who seemed to take a great deal of interest in the stories I was telling about some of the famous people I had worked with. His interest seemed to peak even more so when he noticed how amused everyone was by these stories and how they started to bombard me with questions about my career.

At the very end of the evening, Mr. Thrush asked me if I had ever considered lecturing on the subject of my career and, of course, I told him that it had never entered my mind. He then suggested that I give it some serious consideration and when I offhandedly said that I wasn't sure that I would feel comfortable doing a project like that, he gave his business card anyway and said that if I ever changed my mind he would be more than pleased to handle all of the arrangements and set the wheels in motion for a lecture tour for me.

For the next week or so the thought of lecturing wouldn't leave me, hanging on my subconscious like the grip of an attacking bulldog. I realized that it would take a lot of work on my part to delve into my memories and personal archives to come up with an interesting lecture and, even if I was willing to take this project on, there were still many questions in my own mind that had to be answered before I made my decision. Was I capable of capturing an audience's interest for a minimum of an hour or longer and at the end of my session would any of them be interested enough to ask me any questions? I battled these misgivings for a few more days and then decided to take the bull by the horns. I called Mr. Thrush and, even though he lived up in northern California, we made an appointment to meet in Los Angeles to discuss all the steps needed to get the ball rolling.

As I suspected, it did take an enormous amount of work on my part, organizing exactly what I was going to say and getting together my "show and tell" examples from my archives. Fortunately, I had a marvelous reel of 16mm personal home movies that my guardian took of me and the famous people I had worked with on location and on the Warner Bros. studio lot and this ultimately greatly enhanced my lectures. After getting over my initial nervousness of the first two lecture dates, it turned out to be, and still is, one of my absolute favorite activities. I needn't have initially worried about whether the audience would ask me any questions because ultimately the question and answer period started to extend beyond the time I gave myself for the lecture itself.

One of the times I had a lecture up north, I even did a semi-documentary film on the subject of the wines and winery of the Napa Valley and had the privilege of co-starring in it with Fatty Arbuckle's widow. I treasure the time I spent with Minta Durfee Arbuckle, Charlie Chaplin's first leading lady, and I was completely mesmerized by the stories she told me about the silent era and its stars. At that time there was a possibility that a movie was going to be produced about her life and Minta was bound and determined that I would portray her, but because she was a glamorous lady to the very end and insisted she wear the highest heels that she could, one day she took a very bad fall that ultimately led to her death. I will always treasure her friendship and the tape that I have of her telling of some of her memories of her days in the silent era.

I had been lecturing for over a year when I was booked into a seminar that was sponsored by a woman's club in northern California. The three guest lecturers were going to be Olivia de Havilland, Douglas Fairbanks, Jr., and myself. I was very happy with this booking because it coincided with my birthday, and my husband and daughter were going to fly up with me for the full weekend. Tony had a touch of the flu bug, which was flying around like crazy in L.A., but he assured me that it was not bad enough to stop him from joining us up north.

We all stayed at the home of Mr. and Mrs. Thrush and the evening before my lecture they had planned a big birthday party for me. It was a marvelous party and everyone was enjoying themselves so much, but I was very worried about Tony. He had always been a very strong man, but had the tendency to fluff off any physical discomfort and being the party lover that he was, when he opted to stay in bed rather than join in on the birthday celebrations, I just knew that it had to be something more than just a bad cold. That night neither of us got any sleep because Tony spent most of the time being very sick in the bathroom. The next morning it was all I could do to leave for the theater. However, Mrs. Thrush said she would stay with Tony and see to any of his needs.

The lecture went very well and normally I enjoy doing the question and answer segment, but this time the session seemed inordinately long, and about the only thing that I wanted to do was get back to the Thrush home and see how Tony was doing.

As planned, my daughter and Bill Thrush were waiting at the exit door of the theater lobby and, although the show was over, a few women had stayed behind to get my autograph and compliment me on my lecture. After signing their books and speaking with them a short while, I excused myself as politely as I could and joined Toni and Bill at the exit door. One look at my daughter's face and I knew something was terribly wrong. It was obvious she had been crying, so I looked to Bill for some answers. He told me that Tony had been taken to the hospital in serious condition and that it would be best if he drove my daughter and I straight to the hospital.

As soon as we got to the emergency entrance, I grabbed Toni's hand and we raced into the hospital to try and track Tony down. It was not hard to do as he had just been brought in and was being examined by a doctor in the emergency room. When I was finally allowed to see him, my husband was conscious, but in terrible pain. They had him on an IV and were about to prep him for an emergency operation. Apparently, Tony's appendix had burst some time between our flight to San Jose and my birthday party the night before and it was imperative that they operate immediately because peritonitis had already set in.

During the hours of the operation, the wait was agonizing for Toni and I. We continually held each other's hand, muttering encouraging words to each other, but scared to death for the man we both loved so very much. The entire Thrush family took turns sitting with us and generously offered any kind of help that they could give us, but as much as we truly appreciated their support, it was hard to concentrate on anything but Tony at that time.

When the operation was finally over, the doctor came out to where we were waiting and reported on Tony's condition. He was very straight-forward and told me that Tony was a fighter and had come through the operation but he felt that I should prepare myself for any eventuality be-cause, all things considered, he only gave Tony a 20 percent chance of pulling through. I wanted to scream and run somewhere and just pretend that this was just some nightmare, but with my daughter sitting there beside me I knew I had to take hold for her sake.

I asked the doctor when we could see Tony and he replied that he was now in Recovery, but that he would allow us to see him for just a moment. As we approached the man in bed, for a moment I thought a mistake had been made. My Tony was deeply tanned and although slim of form was decidedly muscular, but this person's face was terribly pale and drawn and the body outlined under the sheet was too small to be that of my six-foot husband. He must have sensed our presence because Tony slowly opened his eyes and although still too groggy to speak, acknowl-edged us with a weak squeeze to our hands. We had only been there a moment or two when a nurse entered the room and told us it would be best for the patient if we left. As reluctant as we were to go, we bent down to kiss him and assured him that we'd see him as soon as he got some needed rest.

The weekend we had so looked forward to had ultimately turned into a two-week stay of anxiety. However in those two weeks my husband proved what an incredible survivor he was because by the time we boarded the plane to take us back to Los Angeles, Tony was very much ambulatory and very anxious to get back to this regular routine. For the first time in about ten days my mind was a bit clearer and I knew that before we left San Jose there was something I had to do.

I sat down with Bill Thrush and his family and thanked them from the bottom of my heart for the love and care they had shown the three of us during a most difficult time, but I explained that after much consideration I felt it best to discontinue my lectures. I further stressed that even though I was never gone for long stretches of time, I didn't want to be separated from my family on a regular basis and this past experience had been a real wake-up call for me. Fortunately, they all understood and we agreed that no matter what happened in the future we would stay in touch with one another.

It was good to get back home. Tony's health improved daily, our daughter was now enjoying her first taste of high school, and I could finally relax and feel that all was right with the world.

Although I was no longer on the lecture circuit, I was still being invited to many industry events and on July 29, 1978, I attended a function at the Screen Directors Guild honoring David Butler for his lifetime achievement as a movie director. The turnout was very good and I found myself getting reacquainted with people I had not seen in years. The biggest surprise of all, and much to my delight, was that one of the attendees was none other than Shirley Temple. Our reunion really stirred up a lot of interest, especially with the photographers, and because they were taking so many pictures of Shirley and I, it was quite a while before we could have a decent conversation. She looked absolutely marvelous and I couldn't help noticing that she was wearing a stunning gold necklace and bracelet. When I commented on it, she told me that both pieces had been presented to her in Africa when she held the post of American Ambassador to Ghana. I was very touched when she told me that she thought of me when she considered visiting my country of South Africa, but had to change her mind because, as Ambassador to Ghana, diplomatically it could have caused a minor problem so reluctantly she put the trip on hold. As warm and pleasant as it was picking up the threads of our past relationship, we both realized that it couldn't happen again anytime soon because Shirley didn't get to southern California that often because her interests lay in politics and therefore Washington and the home she shared with her handsome husband, Charles Black, and their family, in northern California took precedent. As we parted that night, after exchanging home addresses and phone numbers, I couldn't help wondering how long it would be before we met again. Surprisingly enough, it was only five months later.

The Masquers Club was the oldest private show business club in Hollywood and in the first week in December of 1978 they honored Shirley Temple Black with a testimonial dinner and presented her with their highest accolade, the Spelvin Award. The festivities took place in

At the Academy of Motion Pictures, Arts and Sciences. At the cocktail party preceding the presentation of a full-sized Oscar to Shirley on the stage of the Goldwyn Theater. 1985.

the Main Room of the Masquers Club and specifically for this event they added risers to the floor in order to have a proper dais for their honoree and the guest stars who were invited to relate their personal remembrances of Shirley. The organizers had arranged for their honoree and the guest stars to gather in the anteroom just off to the Main Room so that the members of the press would have an opportunity to take pictures of all of us before the main event began. The photographers were in a frenzy trying to line up the best possible shots with Shirley placed front and center, and the rest of us surrounding her. No doubt this was fun time for all of us because there was much giggling and kidding around, and quite reminiscent of a bunch of kids goofing off when the teacher temporarily leaves the classroom.

I'd like to take a moment and comment on what I observed about Shirley that evening. I saw two separate examples of why she was such an ideal person to have a career in the diplomatic service of her country. On the surface she presents a study of a person of reserved authority and yet underneath it all certainly is a most perceptive woman who is sensitive to unspoken feelings and circumstances. That evening when the photographers were trying to line all of us up for a good group shot with Shirley, there were some of us who stood to the side of the room waiting to be properly placed when we noticed that one of our contemporaries, who had always towered in height over most of us, wended her way down to the front and stood next to Shirley, where she apparently felt she belonged. But by this time there were so many people surrounding Shirley I could no longer see her because I am so very short, but I did hear her voice loud and clear. "Sybil, get over here next to me. We shorties have to be up front!" And that's exactly how the picture was taken ... the tall ones in the back and the shorties up in front!

My dinner companion that night was a very handsome and charming actor whom I had never met before. His name was George Montgomery, and he was a terrifically amusing dinner companion in every sense of the word. We were perfectly matched dinner mates because I have a very small appetite and George had a rather large one. A perfect example of our dialogue went this way:

> HE: Are you going to eat that?
>
> SHE: No, would you like it?
>
> HE: Sure would!

This went on throughout the whole main course and when the dessert arrived, his eyes lit up like a Christmas tree. I didn't even reach for my spoon, but gently slid the goody over to his side. As I looked up, I saw a big grin of appreciation on his face and I knew my small gesture had gone over big time with him.

After dinner, introductory speeches were made and then one by one, each of us got up to the lectern to reminisce about how Shirley had played a part in our lives and career. It was obvious that she was a good listener because she had no way of knowing what any of us were going to say, yet after we had related our Shirley stories she made appropriate and sometimes very funny comments that referred to something the speaker had just said. It was during this period that I saw the second example of her sensitivity.

The unfortunate part of a movie career is when the industry rejects an actor because of the age question. It is widely acknowledged that this hap-

Me and Shirley Temple, our first meeting as adults at the Screen Directors Guild in Hollywood.

pens to actresses all of the time but there are many examples of the male actor being shut out of his career for much the same reason. Such was the case of a sensitive and fine actor by the name of Tom Drake. I'm sure everyone remembers Tom as Judy Garland's "boy next door" in MGM's *Meet Me in St. Louis*. In person, Tom was a sweet unassuming man who was as sensitive as the parts he portrayed, but by 1978 Hollywood had not been kind to Tom. Parts were few and far between and when he did work the roles that were given to him could only be described as little more than bit parts.

That evening at the Masquers when it was Tom's turn to speak, he read a poem that he had composed. It was quite beautiful and after he had read it and taken his seat, Shirley responded to his contribution in a warm and compassionate way. She is, for the main part, a very private person and does not give out her autograph or home address very easily, but that night she returned Tom to his leading man status by announcing over the microphone that his poem was beautiful and before the end of the evening she would like to give him her home address so that he could send her a copy of it. After the festivities were over, Tony and I invited Tom to our annual Open House Christmas Eve Party and he was delighted and immediately accepted our invitation. Unfortunately on the evening of our party he phoned us and apologized that he would, with great regret, not be able to come as planned because he wasn't feeling well at all and thought it best to just go over to his sister's home and just take it easy. That was the start of a period of very bad health for him and, sadly, Tom died of cancer not four years later.

In May of 1975, the Academy of Motion Picture Arts and Sciences were going to honor Shirley with a cocktail party and a special film presentation depicting her life and career. Even though I was booked on a flight to New York the next morning to be a guest star at the Al Jolson Centennial weekend celebration, I gladly accepted the Academy's invitation to participate in the festivities.

That evening Tony and I and our daughter Toni entered the front door of the Academy, which at that time was located on Wilshire Boulevard in Beverly Hills, and were surprised to see no signs indicating where the cocktail party was being held. While mulling over what to do next we spotted Charles Black and Shirley's eldest daughter, Susan Agar, waiting for an elevator and we quickly joined them. Charles told us that Shirley was upstairs in one of the banquet rooms, so you can imagine our puzzlement when the elevator doors opened up into a very dark and deserted room. Not knowing what to think, but merely following Charles and Susan to a very small room at the end of the big one, we noticed flashes of bright lights going on and off from its open doorway. As we peeked inside, we saw Shirley and the president of the Academy, Gene Allen, standing on a small platform and a bank of photographers taking pictures of Mr. Allen presenting Shirley with a full sized Oscar in place of the junior one she had received as a child. Obviously the big presentation was going to be held later on in the evening in the Sam Goldwyn Theater, but nobody was supposed to have known about it and I was completely embarrassed about our intrusion on this very private event. As unobtrusively as we could, we started to leave but Shirley spotted us in the doorway and unbelievably stepped down off the platform and came over to greet us. Shirley has such a delicious sense of humor and when I tried to explain away our misadventure, she just giggled with amusement and then tried to make us as comfortable as possible in this very awkward situation. I really appreciated when she took time out to make sure that Toni and Susan were properly introduced but I couldn't wait to get out of there when I saw that Gene Allen was still standing on the platform and the photographers were waiting to resume taking their historical pictures. Shirley gave us some quick directions to get to the cocktail party and said she would be joining everyone in just a few moments. True to her word, she soon greeted all of us who had worked with her and as we traded a few memories with her and each other, the time sped by and before we knew it, it was time to find our seats in the audience-packed Goldwyn Theater. The lights dimmed and on the screen we saw home movies of Shirley before she was Shirley Temple and then progressively they took us on a journey through her life and career. None of us were forewarned that at the end of the film presentation they would show film clips of each of us who had appeared with Shirley in her various movies. It goes without saying my clip with Shirley was from *The Little Princess*, and we all got a round of rousing applause from the audience as each individual clip was shown. When the lights came up, there was Shirley on stage with the very handsome reporter and historian Robert Osborne who acted as moderator for the rest of the evening.

Much to our surprise, each of us was called up individually to relive some of our personal memories of Shirley and although nothing was planned, it all came off very nicely. It was a night to remember and a fitting salute to a much beloved child star.

Generally when one talks of friendship between two women one envisions weekly get-togethers, daily phone calls, shared shopping trips, and keeping in contact via phone and fax machine. I'm proud to say that we have the deepest respect for each other. Nowadays, when television producers want to do a special on Shirley many's the time she has suggested that they get in touch with me as she feels I would be a good spokesperson on the subject of Shirley Temple Black. One day, I told her that I thought it was very sweet of her to make these suggestions, but she simply said, "I trust you." What better compliment can one human being give another?

Twenty years ago, Gary L. Heckman started a Sybil Jason Fan Club and it was to my amazement that it soon became an International Fan Club. In the past few years, I have often been a guest speaker at the California Shirley Temple Fan Club and can lay claim to being made a proud lifetime member by its president, Ruth Pollack. I have become very fond

This was taken on the stage of the Sam Goldwyn Theater at the Academy of Motion Pictures, Arts and Sciences. Bob Osborne, who so often introduces my Warner movies shown on Turner Classic Movies on television, moderates the memories that Shirley and I share working together.

of all its members and especially Ruth, and when she volunteered to become vice president of my fan club I was extremely complimented.

Not too long ago, a young gentleman by the name of Darren Clossin did a drawing of Shirley and me. He rendered it three times so that Shirley and I could sign his copy and keep one each for ourselves. It is a charming drawing, but what fascinated me the most is that he portrayed me as I look in my Warner years rather than in my image of "Becky." The coup de gras was the title he gave to this drawing: FRIENDS ON FILM...FRIENDS IN LIFE.

Yes, He Had An Ego

He was known as the world's greatest entertainer and this was no exaggeration for, as far away as Africa, I remember my father singing Al Jolson songs to me while I was still a baby barely out of the crib. As fate would have it, none of us had ever dreamed that in a few short years I would be in Hollywood co-starring with this icon, in the 1936 Warner Bros. movie *The Singing Kid* and that he and Ruby Keeler would be two of many guest stars appearing in my Technicolor two-reel short called *A Day at Santa Anita*.

There have been quite a number of books written about the life and career of Al Jolson. Two movies, *The Jolson Story* (1946) and *Jolson Sings Again* (1949) were loosely based on his life, so it would be redundant to go into what has already been said so many times before. What I can do is to tell you about my experiences with him first from the viewpoint of a child and then to capture the man once again through the eyes of a young adult. However, I am going to indulge myself in explaining why and how I came up with the title of this chapter.

It has always been a pet peeve of mine that any time people ask me about Mr. Jolson they always add "I understand that he had quite an ego!" Hopefully for the last time, may I say "Yes, he *did* have an ego," but it was also in direct proportion to his generosity. Little, if anything, is said about that. You will see several examples of that within this chapter, and perhaps it will serve to show you a different side of the Jolson you usually read about, the one I worked with and got to know very well.

Long before I was born, Al Jolson was an established entertainer and although I had never seen him perform on the Broadway stage, I have met people who had and they said that they had been absolutely mesmerized by his talent and could not get enough of him. There is no doubt that the stage was his forte and that he had a deep and an abiding monogamous love affair

with his audience, which was emotionally difficult for his wives and lovers. We must never forget that it was he who had made motion picture history by starring in the very first talking picture, *The Jazz Singer* (1927). I honestly believe that he'd be the first person to tell you that he was not much of an actor. but when that man started to sing, everything else fell by the wayside. All of his emotions were wrapped up in song, and that applied to whether he was singing for thousands of people or for just one person.

Many historians insist that by the mid-1930s Jolson's career was all over but the shouting. I saw a different picture of that when, with my own eyes, I saw the fervent enthusiasm of the fans for him at the preview of *The Singing Kid*. My press books are full of great reviews that were written not by the Warner Bros. publicity department, but by the top reviewers of the day and, for the most part, they all agreed that this was his best motion picture to date.

On the other hand, I must admit that there was a slowdown of Al Jolson's career, but not from the lack of interest by the public, but rather by his attitude toward himself. By the mid- to late 1930's, he was quite disillu-

On location with Al Jolson on my birthday, November 23rd, 1936 with a birthday box of chocs. © Turner Entertainment Co., A Warner Bros. Entertainment Inc. Company. All Rights Reserved.

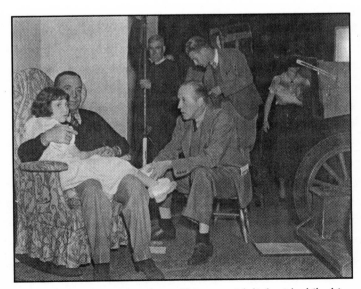

Director William Keighley, Jolie and myself. I was a sick little girl while this scene was shot. Anita's face is blocked by the camera as she gets me a glass of water. © Turner Entertainment Co., A Warner Bros. Entertainment Inc. Company. All Rights Reserved.

On location for *The Captain's Kid*. To the extreme right: Anita with a ribbon in her hair and striped blouse. Ernie Haller is in a sweater vest. © Turner Entertainment Co., A Warner Bros. Entertainment Inc. Company. All Rights Reserved.

sioned with Hollywood, feeling that the movies restricted the natural exuberance which he was able to give vent to on the stage. I suppose he also missed the instant gratification that a performer receives from a live audience. In movies it sometimes takes months before the release of a motion picture and by that time the actor is busy with another project.

It is no secret that Jack Warner idolized Al Jolson, and I seriously doubt he asked for the termination of their contract. Rather, he complied with the actor's request for a release and gave it to him with his deepest regrets. Jolie never again starred in another movie but he did keep busy taking cameo roles in major productions at other studios. I personally think that he was just biding his time until he could return to his beloved Broadway.

That wish became a reality in September 1940 when he opened up as the star and co-producer of a musical called *Hold Onto Your Hats*. Although it played to enthusiastic audiences and garnered glowing personal reviews for Jolson, he soon closed the show. I understand from people who were connected with the production that he felt that his energy level was not at

I adored both Guy and May (she was my neighbor in Beverly Hills). © Turner Entertainment Co., A Warner Bros. Entertainment Inc. Company. All Rights Reserved.

its best and he just wouldn't allow his public to receive anything but his usually high voltage performances. Although he did take some time off to rest, he was not the type to remain idle long so he summoned up some renewed strength and decided to take the show out on tour. After only a brief time, in November of 1941, he not only closed the show once more but closed down the curtain for good on his beloved stage career.

Hollywood is not known to hold out welcoming arms to actors making comebacks, usually predicting dire results for the effort, but in 1946, in an indirect way, Al Jolson proved that theory to be wrong.

Sidney Skolsky, the movie columnist, never lost faith in the magic of Jolson and for a considerable time tried desperately to interest a studio in producing a movie based on Jolson's life. Rejection after rejection greeted his every effort until finally, Harry Cohn of Columbia Studios decided to take a chance and finance Skolsky as producer of *The Jolson Story* and release it through his studio.

While the movie was in production, it became a joke circulating around the inner sanctums of Hollywood. Opinion was that Harry Cohn had at

last lost all of his marbles by financing a movie about a has-been, one who
would be portrayed by an actor who hadn't as yet proven his worth at the
box office. After the release of *The Jolson Story* and its subsequent sequel,
Jolson Sings Again, everyone connected to both productions had the last
laugh. They were both blockbuster hits and deserved the accolades, due
very much to a fine acting job turned in by Larry Parks and the enhance-
ment of the actual singing voice of the legendary star, lip-synced to perfection by Parks. By the time *Jolson Sings Again* was released in 1949, it became
more than just a title for Jolson, because a new generation had discovered
him and now with his new recordings and his own radio show, Al Jolson's
name was once more up in lights.

1936 was a busy year for me. I had just done statewide and Canadian
personal appearance tours, finished the movie *The Captain's Kid*, completed
two of my four Technicolor two-reel shorts, did quite a few radio guest star
shots, and recorded a Decca Sybil Jason Album of Songs, backed up by
Victor Young and his Orchestra. By now my popularity was well established
and Warners were searching around for just the right vehicle for my next
movie. Several possibilities were bandied around but nothing definite had
been scheduled. I had had a good two weeks rest from the personal appearance tour when the studio informed us that my next movie had been chosen and they said that a messenger would deliver a script to us immediately.

The movie was called *The Singing Kid* and to our utter amazement we
were told I would be co-starred with Al Jolson, and supporting us would be
a superb cast. I would have loved to see the look on my father's face when
my parents received our cablegram informing them of this little tidbit! After
all, it had been a comparatively short time since my father had sung Jolson
sings to me in Africa and here was his little daughter about to make a movie
with the Great One!

Over the next few days we were told the rest of the cast and, much to my
delight, I learned that I was going to work once more with the marvelous
character actor, Edward Everett Horton, who had been in my very first Warner
Bros. movie, *Little Big Shot*. Cast as Horton's sidekick would be Allen Jenkins,
who was the nicest, warmest, most genuinely funny actor one could ever
work with. As Jolie's love interest and cast as my aunt would be Beverly Roberts. To round it all off, was the obligatory femme fatale, Claire Dodd, and
two musical greats, Winifred Shaw, and the super kinetic Cab Calloway and
his Orchestra. We were also very much blessed that our songs would be composed by the genius of Harold Arlen and E. Y. "Yip" Harburg, who but three

On the set of *Little Big Shot* with VIP visitors from the New York corporate Warner Bros. offices meeting their new child star and director Michael Curtiz. © Turner Entertainment Co., A Warner Bros. Entertainment Inc. Company. All Rights Reserved.

years later would go on to compose the songs for my friend Judy Garland's classic movie *The Wizard of Oz*.

Much work goes into the planning of a motion picture but when it is a musical, pre-production is monumental. Apart from the usual line learning, wardrobe fittings, makeup and hair sessions, the songs have to be composed and tailored to the stars and the storyline. After that, the music has to be arranged and orchestrated, and the dance routines have to be carefully choreographed by the dance director and taught to the star. Nine times out of ten you record a song with a full orchestra before actually shooting the scene when you go on location. The most obvious reason for this is that it wouldn't be viable to take an orchestra out on location because the noise level from birds, planes, dogs barking, or traffic could disrupt any semblance for clarity of sound. Therefore, the actors record the songs ahead of time and then lip-sync to their own words and music when the scene is shot outdoors.

One usually meets the people you are going to work with on the first

On location on orphanage grounds for *Little Big Shot*, 1935. To the extreme right of
the photo in the background, hanging from the bar in the middle, is the "scared"
real ophan that Curtiz shouted at. © Turner Entertainment Co., A Warner Bros.
Entertainment Inc. Company. All Rights Reserved.

day of shooting on the set, but this was not the case regarding my first
meeting with Mr. Jolson. When the script had been sent to us at home, they
also included the words and music to "You're the Cure for What Ails Me,"
which was the song that would feature Jolie and myself. Fortunately, because my uncle was such a fine pianist, I was able to learn the song ahead of
time, but even then I was still required to come to the studio and rehearse
with the practice pianist because there were certain breaks in the song where
Edward Everett Horton and Allen Jenkins would join in. Then I had to get
used to where the pickup would come in after that. So far I had been the
only one rehearsing with the studio pianist and we assumed that Mr. Jolson
was rehearsing somewhere else with his own personal pianist. One morning
I came in for my usual session, but even before Anita, my uncle and I entered the rehearsal room we heard a lot of laughing going on. As we stepped
through the doorway, we were stunned to see Al Jolson and some other
men standing around the piano enjoying a lively conversation with the pianist. Mr. Jolson spotted us almost immediately and shouted across the

room to me, "Sybilla, come over here and meet your Uncle Al."

When I got to his side, he bent down and gave me a hug, then looked into my eyes and with a big grin on his face said "You gonna do just fine, baby," and then gave me a kiss on the top of my head. He stood up and said, "You wanna sing a song?"

With those words, they initiated our very first rehearsal together. I adored him on sight and there were absolutely no problems connected with our duet...no key changes...no rhythm changes...*nothing*! In fact, after our rehearsal, Mr. Jolson went over to my guardians and said that he was amazed that I had such perfect timing for such a young child and that he got a big kick out of how I picked up on some of his facial expressions.

For a good part of the shooting schedule of *The Singing Kid* I was not feeling too well. Intermittently, I'd get prickly-type pains in the side of my abdomen, and, not being the type of child to complain, even Anita did not know what I was going through. However, one day at home, when I had a day off from the studio, a stab of pain went through me and I grabbed the side of my stomach. My sister noticed this immediately and with great concern asked me why I was holding my tummy like that. I told her what I truly believed to be the truth—that it was only a "stitch in my side." It was a viable explanation, considering that I had been running around and happily tussling with my two dogs for hours, and although Anita accepted it with reservations she warned me that if I ever had "the stitch" again, I was to tell her immediately.

About a week later, we were shooting a scene where the character Al Jolson was portraying was trying to tell me a fairy tale to help put me to sleep, but he got the story all wrong. I then correct his mistakes and by the time I'm through reciting the legitimate version, he has fallen asleep! The director, William Keighley, used a tight two-shot close-up of us sitting in an oversized chair, and while we were waiting for some technicians to make some last minute adjustments, I started to wiggle around in the chair. By now, Jolie knew me well enough to know that I wasn't an antsy-type kid, so he inquired if he was squashing me too much in the chair. When I assured him that it was not the case, he asked me why I was so restless. I told him that I had pains in my tummy. He very gently lifted me out of the chair, stood up, and in a very loud voice said, "See that this child gets some medical attention, and I don't want to see her back here until it's taken care of!"

Anita was frantic with worry and grabbed my hand because she wanted to drive me straight to my doctor's office, but an executive stopped us and

On location for *The Singing Kid*, 1936. To the extreme left I am waiting with Anita
to get ready to join the scene. © Turner Entertainment Co., A Warner Bros.
Entertainment Inc. Company. All Rights Reserved.

said valuable time could be saved if he could escort us to the studio doctor
who was located on the lot, and he could examine me right then and there.
You must understand that at that time, the Warner medical facility was
really nothing more than a first aid station, but it was a fact that the doctor
was certainly knowledgeable enough to diagnose a medical problem. After
my tummy had been poked and prodded, the doctor determined that I was
either having a spasm of the bowel or the start of a problem with my appendix. He felt that at the present moment I wasn't in any immediate danger,
but decided to give me a shot to temporarily ease my pain. He issued me
some pills and cautioned Anita that to be on the safe side, I should not,
under any circumstances, be given a laxative in the next week or two. He
assured Anita that I would be just fine, but if at some future date the pain
recurred, I should then be taken to my personal doctor for a more extensive
examination. Anita never really felt completely comfortable with his assurances, but after two weeks had come and gone and I was free of all pain, we
all relaxed. In retrospect, my sister was so right in her misgivings because it

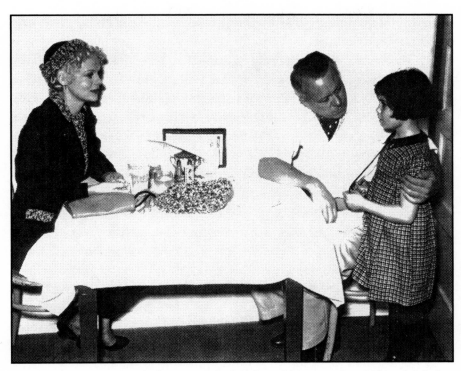

In the "green room" with director Nick Grinde and his very nice girlfriend, Marie Wilson. 1937. © Turner Entertainment Co., A Warner Bros. Entertainment Inc. Company. All Rights Reserved.

wasn't a very long time before we found out that the shot and the pills that the studio doctor had prescribed was a way to numb my pain and stave off an imminent appendicitis attack until the movie was safely in the can.

Two days after the wrap party of *The Singing Kid*, I was at home when I doubled up with pain and was rushed to the hospital. After a quick examination, I was immediately prepped for surgery and no sooner had my own doctor made the incision for an appendectomy, my appendix burst on the operating table!

After the surgery, my hospital was inundated with gifts and flowers, and some of the largest displays came from "Uncle" Al. He never came to see me, but he rang up daily to inquire how I was doing and because he had such a distinctive voice the nurses recognized it and were thrilled to talk to him, if only to give him my progress report. He never missed a day until I was released from the hospital.

I don't want to give the impression that I was miserable all of the time while making *The Singing Kid*. Nothing could be further from the truth.

As long as I can remember I had always worked on my birthdays, and 1936 was no exception.

On November 23, we were scheduled to be on location miles away from the studio, so home and a birthday party was out of the question. Somehow Jolie found out about this and pulled a few tricks out of his hat. On the morning of the 22nd, his assistant called our home and asked Anita to please bring me down to the set for an hour or so in the afternoon. Although I wasn't scheduled to work that day, we arrived at two o'clock and Jolie had just finished doing a scene on the living room set. It's quite the rule of thumb that once a director has OK'd a scene, all the set lighting is shut down. For some reason they remained on. Shading his eyes from the blinding lights, Jolie asked if I was there and when I answered that I was, he asked me to join him on the set. As we stood side by side, he complimented me on what a great job I was doing and how hard I always worked and how badly he felt that tomorrow we'd be on location on my actual birthday. He then said, "Baby, I hope this makes up for it jus' a liddle bit," and out came the most beautiful bike any child could wish for. I was so excited, I could barely talk. Everyone started applauding and whistling and the set photographers took pictures of us with the bike. Apparently, arrangements had been made ahead of time because by the time we got home my wonderful present had been delivered to us. I never stopped riding it around our grounds until it was dinner time and you can believe that I went to bed that night, a very happy child.

The next day at our Franklin Canyon movie location we spent some of the morning rehearsing Jolie's and my duet. Harold Arlen and "Yip" Harburg even drove down to see us perform their song. Luckily. I have 16mm home movies taken that day. As scheduled. we were to shoot the actual sequence right after our late morning run-through. but first the director called for an unusually early lunch break. Before I could eat anything, Anita had to take me into the dressing room to remove my two false teeth caps. Both Al Jolson and I had to wear similar caps because we each had fairly wide gaps between our front teeth. Photographically, that would not have been acceptable in a profession that deemed perfection of image a rule written in stone! As a matter of fact. any time I was not wearing the caps while out in public I soon learned to make sure to smile with my lips closed. You see, there were a lot of things besides learning my lines that I had to remember and when you think about it, it was a lot of responsibility for such a young child.

In the 1930's, location lunches were nothing like the gourmet meals that are supplied to the stars and crews nowadays. Ours usually consisted of box lunches that contained cold fried chicken, sandwiches, a piece of cake, and hot and cold beverages. Imagine our surprise when Anita and I emerged from the dressing room to see that all of the picnic tables had been decorated with colorful tablecloths, balloons, party hats, favors, and everyone was issued small lollipops. To top it all off, scrumptious hot food was served. As if my bike were not enough, Jolie had catered a whole birthday party for this little kid and there was more presents to open up.

At each table there were huge bowls of nice cold punch, but I have the feeling that the ingredients of the one at my table were a wee bit different from the one at Jolie's table because the more that his friends and crew members indulged in the beverage the happier they got!

Mr. Jolson almost always had an entourage of friends with him and they were the nicest men imaginable, but they all looked like characters out of *Guys and Dolls*. Naturally at lunch time they settled themselves down at Jolie's table, and I think what sticks out the most in my memory was the funny sight of these men wearing party harts with lollipops in their mouths and singing a very loud and exuberant rendition of Happy Birthday to me. I think that was probably one of my most memorable birthday parties as a child.

The Singing Kid was not the last time that Al Jolson and I appeared in the same movie. In an earlier chapter I mentioned that I had starred in four Warner Bros. Technicolor two-reel shorts which were produced by Brynie Foy of the famous vaudevillian Foy family. One of the shorts was called *A Day at Santa Anita*. Most of the exterior scenes were shot at the famous racetrack, which was only about two years old at that time, and what made this short so unique is that, in cameo parts, some of Warners' great stars appeared in it, and one of the cutest of these was a repartee between Al and Ruby Keeler discussing his betting techniques. The scenario of the short was basically one of a little girl's love for her horse, but because of the untimely death of her father she is in danger of losing the horse if he doesn't win an important race.

I had no scenes with the guest stars but I did visit the set when Al and Ruby were shooting theirs, and in between scenes we did a lot of joking around. Quite a number of still pictures were taken on the set. Afterwards, we all had lunch in the Green Room and it was hard for me to say "goodbye" to them because I didn't know when I'd see them again.

The next time Jolie and I actually worked together was not long after the theatrical release of *The Singing Kid*. It took place at one of Hollywood's biggest annual social events, the Warner Ball, and it was held in downtown Los Angeles in the magnificent ballroom of the Biltmore Hotel. It was April 23, 1937, and more than a thousand stars, directors and producers attended the affair and were treated to a wonderful show emceed by none other than Al Jolson himself. One of the featured acts was a skit especially written for Jolie and I, and then we segued into our duet of "You're the Cure for What Ails Me." Not only did we get a round of thunderous applause, but garnered a standing ovation. This pleased Jolie so much that just before my exit he hugged me and whispered, "We gottem, baby."

I can't recall the date of our next meeting, but I do remember that it was for a benefit show at the Shrine Auditorium in Los Angeles. A multitude of stars from all of the major studios took part in it, and I am always reminded of that evening each time I see the scene from *A Star is Born* where Esther Blodgett (Judy Garland) meets Norman Maine (James Mason) for the first time backstage at a benefit show.

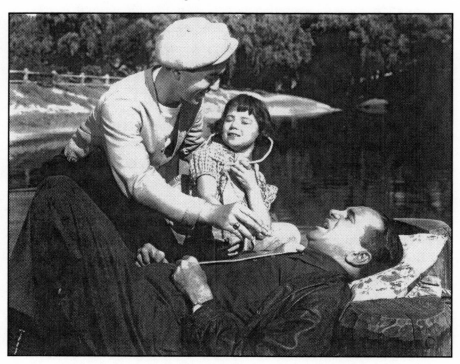

Busby Berkeley directs Al Jolson and myself in our musical number in *The Singing Kid*. He didn't get screen credit. © Turner Entertainment Co., A Warner Bros. Entertainment Inc. Company. All Rights Reserved.

At the opening ceremony of the first day issue of the Al Jolson stamp, attended by many Postmaster Generals. After I unveiled Jolie's stamp, they surprised me by giving me the huge poster of the stamp!

It was just as crowded backstage at the Shrine with stars waiting their turn to go on stage. I remember this particularly well because of an incident that took place not long before being announced on stage. Standing right near me was a man I had never met before. He was eating a bunch of grapes and our eyes happened to meet. He asked me very nicely if I would care to have a grape and being the polite British child that I was I thanked him very much for his offer. He bent down so that I could choose one off of the bunch that he held, and I popped a grape into my mouth. I got quite a shock when I tried to eat it because it was made of wax! I don't know how he did it because he had really been eating them before his offer to me and I had chosen my own grape. He seemed quite pleased at my panic because just then my name was announced on the stage. I quickly spat it out but I remember that Eddie Cantor, who had witnessed this scene, gave him a withering look as I left to go on stage. I can see where W. C. Fields got his reputation for not liking kids!

Although Jolie and I did not team up for this event, we did represent our studio, and at the finale we joined hands and took a final bow at the end of the show.

Al Jolson, Jr. and me at the Al Jolson convention in New York, 1985.

Without a doubt, I think the funniest barbecue I ever attended was at the Encino home of Al and Ruby. The guests were just Anita and myself and another couple with their young daughter. Somehow I got the distinct impression that the Jolsons hadn't been in their home for too long because I overheard Ruby telling my sister and the other woman that there were still a lot of things she still wanted to do with the house. I wish I could remember who the other couple were but they weren't actors. Yet I'm sure they were connected to the motion picture industry. It was very generous of Ruby and Al to have obviously planned for the entertainment of their two little girl guests, for they supplied a generous potpourri of games, dolls, crayons and coloring books, which they encouraged us to take home at the end of the day.

The absolute funniest part of the whole day came when it was time to eat. It was not unusual to see the standard hot dogs and hamburgers, but there were also piles of gastronomical displays of pastrami, bagels, cream cheese and lox, a whole white fish, pickles and olives, potato salad and an eye-boggling array of French pastries! I knew I could always have hot dogs and hamburgers, so I opted to eat a sampling of all those other goodies and I loved every bit of it!

It was many years before I saw Mr. Jolson again. World War II had begun and ended and people were now getting on with their lives. I had already returned to America and was now a young married lady. One morning in May 1950, I was looking through the newspaper and got very excited when I saw that Al Jolson was going to be starring on *Lux Radio Theatre* in a radio version of his movie, "Jolson Sings Again."

I dashed out and obtained two tickets for the broadcast—for Tony and myself. I wound up going by myself because Tony was working at the television station Channel 5 and couldn't get off work. As I waited in line outside of the theater, it occurred to me to write a quick note to Mr. Jolson to let him know that I'd be watching him from the audience. I signaled to the usher who was walking up and down the line to make sure that we were all orderly and not blocking the sidewalk. I asked him if he would please see that Mr. Jolson got my note backstage. At first he was adamant in refusing to take my note, but when I assured him that I knew Mr. Jolson very well and had co-starred with him in a movie, he took it very reluctantly and said he would see what he could do, but he wasn't promising anything. It wasn't long before this young man came running breathlessly back to me in line and said "Mr. Jolson would like to see you in his dressing room, Miss Jason. Would you please follow me and I will escort you there."

When the usher knocked on the star's dressing room door, I must admit I had a sense of panic. I didn't know whether to turn around and run or simply remain there, frozen on the spot. After all, many years had gone by and I didn't know what kind of reception I would receive. I think I would have died if Jolie had just been cooly polite. However when that door opened, I can tell you it was 1936 all over again. He gave me a big bear hug and told me to sit down, make myself comfortable and bring him up to date on what had been happening in my life since the last time we saw one another.

I told him as much as I could and then we got onto the subject of show business. He asked me if I intended on pursuing my acting career, and I said that I was starting to reconsider my decision of retiring. Along with much encouragement on his part, he also cautioned me with some realistic advice. I'll never forget his words verbatim: "Baby, don't lettum get t'ya. Just a short time ago, Jolie couldn't even get a spot on a benefit show—but look at me now. I outlasted 'em all!" He sure did, and I remember thinking then how fortunate we all were that this vibrant man still had many years ahead of him to bring his special magic to us all. In reality, he had only five more

Taken backstage in the Civic Stadium Auditorium for the musical *Jolson*, here are two ladies that manage to see "eye to eye." Leah Segal (Steven Spielberg's mother) and myself.

months to live. On October 22, 1950, he was due to do a radio show with Bing Crosby in San Francisco, but on the night of the broadcast, while he was playing cards with some friends in his room at the St. Francis Hotel, he had a fatal heart attack.

For many years now, the International Al Jolson Society has flown me as a guest star to appear at their various venues across the United States. It is with great enjoyment that I talk about my experiences with Mr. Jolson. This Society has a vast membership all over the world and the name of Jolson is kept alive due to their dedication and love for his singing voice. I personally am very fortunate in that I have some great 16mm home movies that were taken on location during the shooting of *The Singing Kid* and on occasion find pleasure in sharing it with the membership.

Spanning these many years it seems that I am permanently attached to Jolie. On September 9, 1994, I had the honor of unveiling his postage stamp on the day of issue at a large ceremony in Los Angeles. Similarly, in Palm Springs on October 14, 2000, I helped to unveil his star on that city's sidewalk of stars. It was placed right in front of their historic Plaza Theater where Jolson had appeared in the old days.

A few years ago, a musical called *Jolson* opened up in London to great reviews. With different cast members, the show traveled to Canada and then the United States. On October 26, 2000, on the invitation of the producers, I was invited to attend opening night in Pasadena. Apart from enjoying the show, it turned out to be a red-letter night for me because it was then that I finally met Erle Jolson Krasna, Jolie's widow. We had talked several times on the phone but now we were face to face and she turned out to be one of the nicest and warmest ladies I have had the pleasure to meet.

Because we were both guests of the producers, we were invited to meet the star, Mike Burstyn, backstage after the show and it was quite a crush waiting to get into the talented star's dressing room. In the hallway, I was sandwiched in between Erle and a lady that looked very familiar to me. It's rare that I meet somebody as short as I am and she must have been thinking the same thing that I was because we grinned at one another. I was still puzzling where I had seen this lady before, when suddenly it came to me. I took the opportunity to introduce Erle to her. I said, "Mrs. Segal, I'd like to introduce you to the real Mrs. Jolson" and with that, Erle shook the hand of Steven Spielberg's mother, Leah Segal. She in turn introduced us to her charming daughter and we were then ushered into Mike Burstyn's dressing room where a lot of pictures were taken. Both ladies offered me an open invitation to visit with them at any time. I became very friendly with Erle and we shared many a story about Al amidst a lot of laughing. I could easily see how Jolie could have fallen in love with this very warm and gracious woman, so it was with great sadness that I attended Erle's funeral in Beverly Hills on January 16, 2004. It was then I met the rest of her family, two beautiful daughters and a son, plus Al Jolson, Jr., and, like her, they were all a credit to her and her late husband, producer-writer Norman Krasna.

On a final note for those who would still prefer to think of Al Jolson as a selfish and egotistical man, I much prefer to remember him as a generous man with one big gargantuan talent.

Greetings From Hollywood, California, USA

Several times a year I do a number of lectures on my career. At times, when the audience is mostly attended by young men and women in their twenties, I find myself becoming a general historian of sorts. Most of them are already aware of my movie background due to the showings of my movies on television stations such as Turner Classic Movies and the American Movie Classics, but they are very surprised to learn that I am also a veteran of the English Music Hall shows, musical stage plays, records, and many appearances on some of the top flight radio shows done in the 1930s.

I remember at one of my lecture dates a young man took me to task when I used the phraseology of having "appeared on radio." I had to explain that, just like our television shows today, we also had our audiences when we broadcast our radio shows and therefore we "appeared on radio."

There are other similarities that television shares with radio. Each time I drive by the NBC studios in Burbank, California, and see the long lines of people waiting to get into shows like the *Jay Leno Show*, it never fails to remind me of the lineups we had for radio. Just like our popular sitcoms and game shows of today, one had to send away for radio tickets, which sometimes took weeks to arrive in the mail and forced the out-of-towners to plan their vacation time around the dates of those tickets. That didn't seem to affect attendance of the shows because they were always sold out to capacity by enthusiastic audiences.

After the lineup to see the show, the time came to let everyone into the building where all the tickets were scrupulously checked. They were then allowed to enter the inner sanctum of the studio that was carpeted and furnished with luxuriously upholstered theater seats and was in every sense of the word like any plush movie theater of the thirties except that this one was extremely and heavily soundproofed.

If a person came to see a comedy show you were encouraged to enjoy yourself audibly, and strategically placed microphones were suspended on long cords above the heads of the audience to capture their laughter and applause more readily.

However, if it were a dramatic show everyone was warned ahead of time that when they saw the sign light up with the words ON THE AIR, they were encouraged to be as quiet as possible except when they were cued to applaud just before the show went for a commercial break. Yes, we had them in our day too, but they were done live on a separate part of the stage and, at that time, all the microphones in the audience were temporarily shut down except for the ones used by the actors doing the commercial.

The only dramatic shows I ever did, were for the famous *Lux Radio Theatre* and Louella Parsons' *Hollywood Hotel* radio show. This consisted of an edited version of a popular movie, ideally featuring the stars from the movie itself recreating their roles. Generally speaking, when you were a guest star on radio there was a certain decorum practiced that the hardworking radio soap opera stars didn't have to observe and that was in the matter of dress.

Because the soap opera people didn't perform in front of audiences, they could come into the studio dressed in any manner they wished, but we, on the other hand, came decked out in finery befitting stars of the silver screen because the fans expected no less from us. Sometimes it was strangely incongruous, especially when we were portraying people of poverty, but we were giving the public what they wanted and that was all that mattered in the long-run.

For quite a while most of the major radio shows emanated from New York, but as time went by, some of it filtered down to southern California to take advantage of the easy accessibility to movie stars and the great comedians like Jack Benny and Eddie Cantor and their contemporaries who all had national appeal. I did guest shots on both coasts and remembering back some of them were a lot of fun to do. It didn't seem like work at all. Three of those especially come to mind.

When I was just a little one starting out in show business, I became quite well known for my imitations of stars like Maurice Chevalier, Greta Garbo, Mae West and Jimmy Durante. In 1937 on James Melton's *Sunday Night Party* radio show in New York, I had the honor of being co-

The Three Musketeers at their first meeting: Peggy Ann Garner, myself and Edith Fellows. We truly were one for all and all for one!

starred with Mr. Durante, and the writers took full advantage of the fact that I could imitate the Schnozzola by writing us a special skit called "Durante and Jason," and a song that we both sang in the Durante voice. The audience loved it and because Jimmy was obviously getting a kick out of a little kid imitating him he often broke up with laughter. It became extra enjoyable for everyone.

In June of 1955, Jimmy was doing a television show at NBC in Burbank, California, and I went to see it. I had previously let the producers of the show know that I would be in the audience and would love to see their star after the show. They were kind enough to make arrangements so that I could go backstage after the telecast. I don't know how he did it but Jimmy recognized me right off the bat, gave me a hug and said "Yer still as cuuute as a button, but ya didn' grow much taller than upta hya!" and he pointed to his famous nose. Unfortunately, we didn't have too much time together because Mr. Durante was surrounded by reporters like Sheila Graham who were due to interview him in his dressing room. I found him to be just as sweet and warm as I had remembered him, those many years ago. However, I can't say the same thing about Sheila Graham.

For the short time Jimmy and I talked, Miss Graham did not try to hide her annoyance at being kept waiting and she tried to interrupt our reunion several times. Being the gentleman that he was, Mr. Durante eased the situation by saying, "You remember Sybil Jason, don't you, Sheila?" and she replied in a very disinterested way, "I'm not sure." I could tell that her attitude embarrassed him, but because other reporters were also waiting for him he reluctantly gave me a parting hug and apologized for having to leave and expressed the hope that we could meet at a more opportune time at some later date and talk over old times. I believed the man was as genuine as an unflawed diamond and meant what he said, but unfortunately that meeting never happened!

As for Sheila Graham, whom I am not going to let off the hook, in her column in the *Citizen News,* she wrote about her interview with Jimmy, and she even mentioned my name. Instead of reporting that the beloved comedian had reintroduced us, she wrote that I had approached her and asked whether she remembered me, to which she wrote, "And, of course, I didn't!" How strange of her to have written that, considering that in 1936 I had owned a house on Whitley Terrace in the Hollywood Hills and my neighbor was none other than Miss Graham. We used to wave to one another almost daily and my guardians and I used to see her lover, F. Scott Fitzgerald, the famous writer, coming and going from her home on a regular basis. She was just starting to get a foothold as a gossip columnist and in that year of 1936 found it "quite a feather in her cap" to get an interview with "the brilliant child star, Sybil Jason." That was her quote, not mine. How soon they forget!

The second radio show that I had fun doing took place in New York in 1937. Rudy Vallee, who had been a famous singer for more years than you could count, requested me as one of his guest stars on his April 29th radio show. I got very excited for four particular reasons. Of course, I liked very much Mr. Vallee who, years later, became a regular guest our home, but when I heard who the other guest stars were going to be, I could hardly wait to do the show. For starters, three of those people consisted of the genius ventriloquist Edgar Bergen and his two lovable creations, Charlie McCarthy and the country bumpkin, Mortimer Snerd. I was a big fan of the three of them, and rarely missed their radio show, so when I read the script for the Vallee program I knew that I was going to have the opportunity to "converse" with them.

I must explain the amazing thing about these little characters. They had equal appeal for both adults and children and because Bergen's own writers were so very good, Charlie and Mortimer came across as totally human and at times one forgot that they were just dummies. To digress for just a moment, there is an absolutely delicious story about when Edgar Bergen first came out to Hollywood with Charlie and Mortimer to audition for a part in Sam Goldwyn's upcoming production of *The Goldwyn Follies*. Although I can't personally vouch for its authenticity, the story is just too priceless to pass up.

The test scene was shot on the Goldwyn lot and because the script had been taken from one of Bergen's own radio shows, the familiarity of the dialogue assured that it would be a quick and uncomplicated shoot. Once it had been completed, Bergen was satisfied that the test had gone well and he sat back for a few days to await the results. As his want, Sam Goldwyn liked to keep a sharp eye on his studio's expenses and, as fate would have it, before he had had the chance to view the Bergen test, the expense sheet for it had been placed on his desk. Horrified, he saw that the simple scene had cost more than any other in the studio's recent history, so picking up his phone, he ordered that the test director come to his office immediately and explain the reason for the horrendous expense that was expended for that test.

When the director arrived, Goldwyn wasted no time in pointing to the cost sheet, and very sheepishly, the director said that they had had a sound problem which led them to shoot the scene over and over again. He further explained that none of them could figure out what the problem was because the soundman had checked out every inch of his equipment and found everything to be in topnotch working order. All they could do was just keep on trying to get a good sound fix and that ended up costing a lot of time and money before they finally solved the problem near the end of the day.

On a motion picture set, a boom man is the one who handles a microphone that is suspended on a long pole above the heads of the actors, out of camera range. It is imperative that the mike be directly overhead of the person who is speaking at that particular moment. In the case of the Bergen test, the boom man had become so entranced with the repartee between the ventriloquist and his famous sidekicks, that he forgot that they were merely dummies, and each time they "spoke," instead of staying with Bergen, he would swing the mike over to above the heads of Charlie and Mortimer! Sam Goldwyn probably didn't appreciate the humor in this but if the story is true I think it's a priceless piece of Hollywood history.

I have already mentioned that there were four good reasons I was so thrilled to do the Vallee show. Now you know that three of them were Edgar Bergen, Charlie McCarthy and Mortimer Snerd. However, I was completely in awe of the star who made up the fourth person, excluding myself, involved in the comedy skit. Although we both worked for Warner Bros., I had never met the gentleman before and he was and is, to this day, my absolute favorite character actor of all time.

Two days before the show was to air, we all met at the radio station for rehearsals and I could not believe that I was actually reading lines with the great Claude Rains! As young as I was, I had always been a complete professional in my work and was even tabbed "One Take Jason," but now I absolutely lost my cool when Claude Rains was conversing with the country bumpkin Mortimer Snerd. The actor played it just as straight as if he were doing a scene with his oft-time leading lady, Bette Davis. Of course, this made it all the more hysterically funny. Right in the middle of one of his lines, I couldn't contain myself and started giggling like crazy. Then I saw him look at me, raise his one eyebrow as if to say "get a hold of yourself, young lady." That quickly brought me back down to earth, and I was so grateful when we aired the show that I had gotten it out of my system because the audience had the same reaction that I had at rehearsals.

After the show was over, everyone seemed pleased at the results and as we all said our goodbyes, I saw Mr. Rains coming toward me. When he reached my side he gave my arm a gentle pat and with his mouth positioned in its distinctive sideways smile he said, "You were very good" and then turned on his heel and slowly walked out of my life. He had only uttered four little words to me, but I felt like I had just won the Academy Award!

The third radio show stands out in my memory because it was done in such a different way, and for a very unique reason. Up until that time, it was going to be the most historic program ever aired, although in this present day and age it might seem very archaic. It was a wonderment on April 17, 1936. For the very first time, a radio program emanating from Hollywood, California, was going to be heard instantly by millions of people in South America, and they were going to be greeted by some of Hollywood's most renown personalities.

The officials of the newspaper *La Critica* had arranged for the hookup, which traveled 8,500 miles over land wires and air waves before it was released over a radio station in Buenos Aires. According to the news releases of the day, electrical impulses traveled at the speed of light and within a fraction of a second we were heard by more than 25 million people in South America. The amazing thing is that although all of this happened in the blink of an eye, the program was sent on quite a circuitous route. Beginning in Hollywood, it was sent to New York via telephone lines and then from New York on a special shortwave channel to rebroadcast in Buenos Aires.

Those were the technical aspects of the program, but on that morning in Hollywood one could feel the excitement that was generated when 34 of us arrived at the radio station. We had all been pre-warned that this event would take the better part of the day, starting with rehearsals and then the actual broadcast, but even though everyone was aware of the importance of taking part in a historical event, the atmosphere and mood was very light and festive.

When we first arrived at the studio, we were given instructions on what was expected from all of us, but we were also told to just relax because throughout the morning we would be called up to the microphone individually or by twos and threes to rehearse our lines with the emcee. The remaining guests were then free to socialize with their fellow actors and to partake in the day-long offering of food and drink catered for the comfort of the celebrities involved in the program. And what a lineup it turned out to be. Very appropriately, our master of ceremonies was Leo Carrillo, so well remembered in movies and then on television as Pancho, the sidekick of The Cisco Kid. Leo spoke in both Spanish and English that day and for the entertainment segment of the show Francis Lederer, Bing Crosby, Dixie Dunbar and Walt Disney's Mickey Mouse characters put on a sketch with music and song.

Throughout the broadcast, the people of South America heard hearty salutations given by the likes of producers Jesse Lasky, Jack Warner, and the famous German producer-director Max Reinhardt, and they were joined by some of Hollywood's brightest stars. For my part, I gave my greetings in English but had phonetically learned a short sentence in Spanish as did some of the rest of the celebrities.

The roster included Mary Pickford, Claudette Colbert, Billie Burke (a.k.a. Mrs. Florenz Ziegfeld and, three years later, the good witch Glenda in *The Wizard of Oz*), Jackie Cooper, Fred MacMurray, Virginia Field, Jeanette MacDonald, Gene Raymond, Clark Gable, Barbara Stanwyck, Claire Trevor, Jean Hersholt (his nephew is Leslie Nielsen), Anita Louise, Merle Oberon, Ginger Rogers, Olivia de Havilland, Anne Shirley, Keye Luke, and Jack Oakie.

As a rule, children are very perceptive in forming opinions of the people that they meet, for the simple reason they haven't as yet been corrupted by outside influences. On that day, and being in the midst of such a large group of people, I had ample opportunity to form my own impressions. As I now run through the list of attendees, I see that although I had met a good percentage of the stars on previous occasions, it was exciting to meet the others whom I only knew through seeing their movies.

Going back to 1935, when I first arrived in Hollywood, my sister, my uncle and I had had the privilege of being invited to the home of Mary Pickford. Let me say that invitations to her famous estate, Pickfair, were rare and very selective, but I believe there were two reasons why we were invited. First of all, both Miss Pickford and her husband were staunch Anglophiles, and me being a little English girl helped a lot. But I think the capper was that before Jack Warner had ever brought me over to Hollywood, I had a small part in a British-made movie which starred her much younger husband, actor and bandleader Buddy Rogers.

I found her to be very sweet and uncomplicated and obviously enjoying her life away from the camera, although she was very busy as a board member of many Hollywood and charitable organizations. I remember the time I shared a private box with Miss Pickford and Charlie Chaplin at an ice skating show starring Sonja Henie. Because I was a devotee of ice skating shows, and am to this day, I was one thrilled little girl when I was chosen that night to present Miss Henie with an enormous bouquet of roses, at the finale of the show.

The most fascinating charity event I attended was one that Miss Pickford captained on May 4, 1962. It was for the Motion Picture Relief Fund and it was held at the pre-opening of the MovieLand Wax Museum in Buena Park right near Disneyland. The champagne buffet dinner was served to all of us under a humongous size tent on the grounds of the museum and the guest stars spanned many eras that night. It was fascinating to talk to some of the greats of motion pictures starting with Francis X. Bushman, who co-starred in the original *Ben-Hur*. It progressed all the way up to the current stars of the 60's.

Mary Pickford was a tireless worker for so many worthy charities and it was a great loss to all of them when she passed away in 1974 at the age of 86 years old. After her demise, I saw Buddy on numerous occasions at banquets where we, amongst others, were honored for our contributions to the entertainment industry. Although we have also lost Buddy, he too lived to a ripe old age and he led a productive life right up to the very end.

Another star at the historic radio broadcast was Claudette Colbert. I had met her several times before because my sister Anita was a member and a volunteer at Miss Colbert's favorite charity and over the course of time Miss Colbert prevailed upon Anita to let me appear as a celebrity at one of her fund raisers. One of these was an outdoor party held on the grounds of Miss Colbert's home and I remember this day distinctly because for the majority of that afternoon one of the star guests, who was a very tall and quiet young man, joined Anita and I and never left our sides until the end of the party. Of course, we were the envy of every young lady attending the party that day and any one of them would have gladly traded places with us just to keep company with the very masculine but very shy...John Wayne!

I had never met Billie Burke before the day of the broadcast and although she frequently portrayed rather flighty and empty-headed women in her movies, she was nothing like that in person. She was quite beautiful and it was easy to see what a man like Florenz Ziegfeld, whose trademark was featuring beautiful young women in his Broadway shows, saw in Miss Burke whom he ultimately married. The day of the broadcast I noticed that although she quietly remained in her seat while others circulated around the studio, a steady stream of celebrities went up to her and seemed to be paying her homage. She was charming to everyone, yet obviously was quite embarrassed by all the attention being paid to her. When I was introduced to her, she took my hand in both of hers and she gave it a gentle squeeze. What impressed me most about her was her genuine warmth and the kind expression in her eyes. I never met her again, but years later her daughter, Patricia Ziegfeld, wrote about me in her newspaper column.

Jackie Cooper was a contemporary of mine and although we never made a movie together, we did share some guest spots on radio shows and personal appearances at other show business functions. He is a few years older than I, and like boys at that age, he didn't have too much time for girls.

For a number of years, I used to visit Glenda Farrell at her home. This was long after we had made the movie *Little Big Shot* at Warners. It was especially exciting on the Fourth of July, because she always arranged to have a spectacular fireworks display in her backyard to entertain her family and friends.

Occasionally I would wander into their playroom and watch the two boys play the drums and I'm sure had Jackie not been an actor he would have made it as a professional drummer. He was that good at it. Years later it came as no surprise to me to learn that when he joined the navy in World War II, he played the drums in the Armed Forces band that traveled around and entertained the troops. I don't know whether it was because of the disparity in our ages, but I always found Jackie to be a bit introverted and hard to relate to but regardless of that I personally believe that he was one of the most talented of the boy child stars. I would have loved to have met all of the stars at the radio station that day, but logistically it wasn't feasible given that we were scattered around in different groups.

Sometimes it's hard for the public to realize that the stars themselves are the biggest fans of their contemporaries, and are just as thrilled to meet them as are the general public. That day I never got to meet Fred MacMurray, Virginia Field, Jean Hersholt, or Keye Luke, but I did feel very fortunate to have met all of the others.

For instance, one would be hard put to find a more charming couple than Jeanette MacDonald and Gene Raymond. He was very handsome, full of life and obviously very much in love with Miss MacDonald. It was easy to see why she had attained stardom because, along with her magnificent singing voice, she had that certain kind of magic. Wherever she went, all eyes would be drawn to her beauty and magnetic personality. Another fascinating fact about Jeanette MacDonald is that although she carried herself like royalty she was completely approachable. I spent quite a time talking to them, but never once did I feel that they were bored being in the company of a child. I was fascinated with her eyes. Apart from the fact that they were quite beautiful, they twinkled like she was enjoying some funny but private joke yet, in a moment's notice, if the subject turned to something sad, the expression in her eyes changed to deep compassion.

In my adult years, Clara Rhodes, who was president of the Jeanette MacDonald Fan Club for many years, invited me be one of their annual guest speakers and it was my pleasure to talk about my memories of Jeanette and Gene. Of course, by then, Miss MacDonald had long ago passed away, but Gene always attended these functions and the banter back and forth between he and Clara Rhodes was just hilarious. We lost Gene a few years ago and although the last time that we saw him he was in a wheelchair and quite frail, he attended these banquets up to the very end. His humor was still very much intact. Sue Garland, who has now taken the helm of the club, has extended the invitation to me and Tony to attend their gatherings and it is still my pleasure to relate my experiences about both Jeanette and Gene.

I have mentioned previously that Clark Gable had been edited out of my two-reel short *A Day at Santa Anita*, but that day at the radio station I finally did get to meet him. Let me tell you, he was a sight to behold. I think what I remember most about him were his dimples, his charming smile, his huge hands, and no...I didn't think his ears were particularly large, but maybe they did stick out a bit more than is usual. He was very nice to me, but I do think that he was out of his element in the company of a child because he had a rather sheepish look on his face when we were introduced and shook hands. He was the very first person ever to call me honey and because I was still very much a little English girl not familiar with all American expressions, in private I asked Anita if that was a compliment and she assured me that it certainly was! In body size, Clark Gable was not overwhelmingly big in the sense that John Wayne was, but he had a certain knockout charisma that worked full voltage on every female in the studio that day. In hindsight, who better to have portrayed Rhett Butler in *Gone With the Wind*?

There were two popular women stars who took part in the program that day, and although they often shared the same kinds of roles as tough ladies or girlfriends of mobsters, one of them didn't seem to have to stretch her acting ability very far to portray these characters. The first lady was Claire Trevor and although I never worked with her, I often saw her on the Warners lot and she never failed to give a ready smile to me or to anyone passing in her direction. We sat next to each other for a good part of that day and she couldn't have been nicer had I been an adult. She had a warm personality and displayed genuine interest in what you were saying, and punctuated that interest by giving you her rapt attention. She had a great sense of humor and told me some funny things that had happened to her in her daily life and on the set. To this day, I wish that I could have worked with this very talented lady.

The lady sitting on the other side of me was, no doubt, a popular star, but I don't think she said two words to anyone that day. Barbara Stanwyck had brought reading material with her and just kept to herself until it was her time up at the microphone. Right after that, she left the studio. Hopefully, Miss Stanwyck was just having a bad day and was quite different at other times.

I found Merle Oberon to be a very mysterious and fascinating lady. She seemed a bit introverted, or maybe shy would be a better word to describe her, but whenever she did smile her whole face seemed to light up. I'm sure that, unlike Miss Stanwyck, Miss Oberon really enjoyed being in the company of other talented and interesting people because years later she was known to throw some of the most fabulous and lavish parties here and abroad, getting the well-deserved reputation of being a superb international hostess. Except for my blue eyes and her brown ones, we resembled each other. When I was quite young, I was requested to test for the part of Merle as a young girl in the classic movie *Wuthering Heights,* but Darryl Zanuck wouldn't loan me out because I was under contract to his studio, Twentieth Century-Fox.

I knew Anita Louise during the period when she was in the midst of making the Warner Bros. epic *A Midsummer Night's Dream,* and although that day at the radio station we were both taking part in the broadcast, I only got to really know her when we were both cast in the Shirley Temple movie *The Little Princess.* As you saw Anita Louise in that movie, so she was in person, a lovely delicate and warm woman. Although she and I didn't have many scenes together in *The Little Princess,* off camera she and my sister and I spent a lot of time talking about our days at Warner Bros. I was very fond of her and was quite distressed to learn years later that she had had some bad personal problems that led to a drinking problem and ultimately led to a much too early death.

Imagine my astonishment that day at the station when Ginger Rogers, whom I had never met before, walked over to where I was sitting and told me that she was delightfully surprised when she went to see *Little Big Shot* and heard me sing her name in one of my songs in that movie. She said it had been the first time that had happened to her. I'm sure since then this has happened numerous times, but in retrospect I have often thought what a gracious thing to have done by putting herself out just to compliment a child.

When I first met Olivia de Havilland she had just started filming *A*

Midsummer Night's Dream at Warners and although she was still in her teens and still very prone to blushing and shyness, she also was a keen observer and most aware of every aspect that went into becoming a star.

One day in 1937, a series of publicity shots was being taken of me by one of the top-flight Warner Bros.' still photographers and we happened to be shooting them on a hillside on Barham Boulevard, which was just a stone's throw away from the studio. That piece of property now belongs to Universal Studios, but in the thirties, Barham Boulevard was not the busy thoroughfare that it is today so it wasn't unusual to be able to park one's car on the soft shoulder of the road.

When Olivia happened to drive by and saw all the activity of the photo shoot, she pulled up to the side of the road and joined my sister in observing what we were doing. In between shots, Olivia asked many technical questions of our photographer and because of this enquiring habit of hers, I'm sure it stood her in very good stead for her future years in show business. Apart from appearing as one of my guest stars in the short *A Day at Santa Anita*, we never made a movie together, but I often saw Olivia when we both attended movie premieres or took part in benefit shows or occasionally ate lunch at Warner Bros. on the lot café called the Green Room. That was about the extent of our relationship because one must remember that I was still a young child and Olivia was well on her way to becoming Errol Flynn's leading lady and making her mark in Hollywood history. However, before that happened, we did the radio broadcast to South America, and anyone who was there that day could see that Olivia was delightfully enthusiastic and was as thrilled as I was to meet all the rest of the celebrities.

In an earlier chapter I wrote about when Olivia, Douglas Fairbanks, Jr. and I were booked into a theater in northern California to do lectures on our careers. We didn't share a stage, but were presented on different days so we didn't have a chance to bump into each other. A couple of years later, in Hollywood, we were just two of many stars who were honored guests at the 50th anniversary celebration of sound in movies. It was an exciting event that started on the original soundstage where Al Jolson made *The Jazz Singer*. After that, special transportation took us over to the Hollywood Palladium where comedy writer-producer Hal Kanter and President of the Motion Picture Association, Jack Valenti acted as emcees and introduced all of us individually that day. As a matter of fact, everyone got a big laugh when Hal Kanter introduced me. He was very com-

PROBLEM PICTURE. We put this in for fear you might be tired of all the love stuff. Among those present are Leo Carrillo, Merle Oberon, Francis Lederer, Olivia De Havilland, Jeanette MacDonald, Gene Raymond, Anita Louise, Jackie Cooper and Sybil Jason. Try and identify

At the historical radio broadcast where for the first time ever a program coming from Hollywood went directly to Buenos Aires. This was just one of many group stills taken that day.

After a historical radio broadcast. Jack Oakie discovers little Sybil is all grown up!

At the historical radio broadcast, left to right: Jack Oakie, Broadway star Winifred Shaw, Claire Trevor. Back row: Barbara Stanwyck and newcomer John Garfield. In the dark at left: Max Reinhardt and Mary Pickford.

plimentary and then said "... and Sybil was Jack Warner's first child ... (a long pause) star!" That day was wonderful for me personally because I got the opportunity to talk to so many stars and directors I had worked with when I was a kid but had not seen in years. Olivia and I talked for a short while, but it wasn't quite the same. I was now an adult and she was a world renown star who had acquired a sophisticated and somewhat hard veneer, and I must admit I sorely missed the young and enthusiastic Olivia but at the same time I realize that it's natural for people to move on in life and for her this was a natural progression.

One of my favorite memories of her was in 1939 when I was on the guest star list to attend the glamorous Hollywood premiere of the historic movie *Gone With the Wind*. As one of the stars of that epic, I don't think I have ever seen Olivia look quite as beautiful as she did that night at the Carthay Circle Theater in Beverly Hills. Throughout the years she has gained a well-earned reputation as a fine dramatic actress in such films as *The Snake Pit, To Each His Own, The Dark Mirror* and *The Heiress,* but I think in the minds and hearts of the general public she will always be fondly remembered for her Oscar-nominated performance as the delicate and sensitive Melanie in *Gone With the Wind*. For many years now Olivia has made her home in France.

I have to smile as I write about the last person on my list from that historical broadcast day. I had never met Jack Oakie before and never did again until many years later. But on that day, we had our picture taken along with Claire Trevor and singing star Winifred Shaw, who was featured in a musical production number in *The Singing Kid*.

In my memory, Oakie stands out clearly just like a delighted child who was locked in a candy store. The "candy" in this case were all the beautiful lady stars, but also included the public relation girls and the food caterers. How that man loved the ladies and, as long as he didn't overstep his boundaries as he did on occasion, they all got a kick out of him. I had a good giggle when I overheard a comment that Wini Shaw made to Claire Trevor, and even though I don't think I understood the full concept of the remark, it did seem very funny to me. "Oakie reminds me of a psychotic bee flitting from flower to flower!"

Many, many years later, at a banquet honoring a lot of us from the Golden Era of Hollywood, a newspaper photographer asked Jack and I to pose together, which we did. About a week later, the photographer was kind enough to send me copies of those pictures which just happened to be three time-lapsed shots of the two of us. Looking at them and knowing the full story, it clearly told a tale of discovery, rejection, and finally, redemption. In the first shot, Jack must have suddenly come to the realization that I was all grown up and now he was entitled to explore my adult bottom. As a result, in that first shot, you will see a glazed expression on my face and a big grin on his. In the second shot, I am tickling him and he is laughing hysterically, which I had hoped would keep his hands occupied and away from my rear end. Before the third shot, when someone came up to the photographer and talked to him for a moment, I had just enough time to ask Jack to act like the gentleman that I was sure he was...and he did! The last photo turned out to be a lovely one of both of us, and one of which I have kept to this day.

Little Stories About Big People
What Kind Of Sandwich Did You Eat?

Christmas has always been a magical time for children all over the world, but never more so than in the almost mythical land of Hollywood in the 1930's and 40's. Of course, we didn't have the advantage of television, so that everyone got the benefit of witnessing our spectacular local parade, but if you were lucky enough to live in southern California, or could afford to come out here for the Christmas season, then you could stand on Hollywood Boulevard in near perfect weather, and watch Hollywood produce its magic.

As much fun as it is nowadays to watch what is now called the unimaginative title of the Hollywood Christmas Parade, it pales in comparison to the glamorous and certainly more charming Santa Claus Lane of my era. It is true that in recent years the public enjoys watching the appearance of popular sitcom and soap opera stars, which are interspersed with radio disc jockeys and politicians, but you will find a major scarcity of movie stars, which is rather strange considering this parade takes place in the so-called motion picture capital of the world!

To give you an idea what it must have been like in the past, try to imagine watching car after car go by, contained such mega-stars as Harrison Ford, Julia Roberts, Tom Cruise, Brad Pitt, Meg Ryan and Tom Hanks, to name a few, and you'll get the feel of the glamour and excitement of the Santa Claus Parade.

To herald the event, one could see for miles around the broad beams of light in the sky that emanated from the huge klieg lights that swung from side to side. When the actual ceremony was to begin, the honorary celebrity would pull a switch, which lit up all the lampposts on the boulevard that had been transformed into three-dimensional Christmas trees just for the holidays. I have seen some archival black and white footage covering this event, but it comes across as very bland and doesn't give one the true representation of the colorful and glamorous event that we all experienced.

Hollywood didn't stop promoting the Christmas season, even when the Santa Claus Lane Parade was over. Every night, until Christmas Eve, at a specific and well-publicized time, Santa's float would go down Hollywood Boulevard and he would share his vehicle with a famous star. If for some reason you were not aware of this event taking place, you couldn't miss hearing the loud electronic HO HO HO that would reverberate for blocks around. Neither Santa nor Hollywood was ever shy about making their presence known at all times.

As I have mentioned previously, I do not remember not working on my birthdays or holidays, and Christmas was no exception. Yearly, about a week away from Christmas Day, Warners would arrange a special matinee strictly for kids at their Hollywood Boulevard theater and I was always expected to entertain them on stage. A master of ceremonies would interview me and ask questions that kids would typically be interested in, and then, accompanied by an orchestra, I would sing "Santa Claus is Coming to Town," which was the perfect cue for Santa to join me on stage. The kids would hoot and holler with excitement because they knew from past experience that every single one of them would be handed a gift-wrapped present from Santa and me. It's hard to imagine, considering the large seating capacity of the theater, how it was handled in such an orderly manner. Someone very wise had figured out that by calling out different age groups, like from five to seven years old, and then splitting them up into boy-girl categories, we were able to go through the whole audience and not one child lost out on a suitable present.

One Christmas, another little girl a few years older than myself, joined me up on the stage to sing "Santa Claus is Coming to Town," and it is amazing how well we did considering we had never met before, much less sung together. We got along so beautifully that after the show was over we posed for photos outside of the Warners theater with our arms around each other's waist. We begged everyone that we be allowed to have lunch together. We did and it was a nonstop laughing session. She had not reached star status at that time, but that was not long in coming. I only saw my new friend just a few times after that, but it seemed like with each succeeding meeting, the ebullient girl that I had sung with on the Warners stage had changed. Judy Garland seemed old beyond her years and the ready laughter that I remembered bubbling out of her was now very slow in coming. By the time I went to a party that was held at MGM for their child star Freddie Bartholomew's birthday, it seems with the progression of Judy's popularity came the unfortunate regression of her off screen persona. I am not going so far as to say she was in a state of depression, but there was a definite and sobering change in her.

In the various Christmas parades I was in, I shared sitting with Santa on his float with other child stars.   One time it was Anne Shirley who, although historians rarely mention her, was enormously popular at that time. Anne was about seventeen then and just about to graduate into the young leading lady status. She retained her popularity for quite a while until she decided to voluntarily retire from acting. It no longer held any interest for her and she must have made the correct decision because she went on to lead a very happy life with her third husband, screenwriter Charles Lederer.

On one of those Santa rides, I was delighted when I saw that it was going to be Judy and I who would be riding with Mr. Claus on his float. She would be seated on his right side and I would be seated on his left, and in this way the people on both sides of Hollywood Boulevard would be able to get a good view of at least one of us and a partial view of the other. At that time, all parade vehicles were stationed on an empty lot on Vine Street just bordering Sunset Boulevard. By schedule, one by one, all of the vehicles left that lot and wended their way slowly up to Hollywood Boulevard where they would take their place in line to join the parade.

That evening when Judy and I were waiting to board the float, she asked me if I had eaten anything as yet. I told her that I had had a tiny sandwich before we left home because I understood that we were going to be fed after the parade and I didn't want to spoil my appetite. She looked at me very sadly and asked what kind of sandwich did I eat at home. I thought it was a rather strange question, but I answered it and before we could say another word it was time to board the float.

As we headed down Hollywood Boulevard, Judy waved to her side of the street and I did the same on mine, while Santa was kept busy throwing tiny candy canes down to the public from the enormous sack on his back. After a little while, I looked at Judy and I couldn't believe what I was seeing. As fast as she could unwrap those tiny candy canes that she took from Santa's sack, she would shove them in her mouth and devour them. This went on til the end of the parade. Poor dear must have known what was coming because, if I remember correctly, it was at the Hollywood Roosevelt Hotel we were taken to after the parade, for our dinner. It was one of those buffet-type dinners where you served yourself, and as Judy and I approached the food tables we saw this plethora of delicious dishes that were set out for everyone who had taken part in the parade. Grinning at each other in anticipation of these goodies, Judy and I got our plates and were just about to choose what we wanted for dinner when a man came over to us, took Judy's plate away from her and led her back to our table. My food stuck uncomfortably in my throat that night as my friend sat there with just a glass of water in front of her. If I had to guess, I believe that man was from MGM and was probably there to keep an eye on her and make sure she didn't eat anything. The studio didn't want her to get fat and was adamant that she stick to an unrealistic diet!

The next time that I saw Judy, I was preparing to do *The Little Princess* at Twentieth Century-Fox and she was about to do a movie that would make her an icon for all time, *The Wizard of Oz.* We were guests at a party for a famous lady author of children's books and after we had posed for the mandatory publicity pictures, we were able to take a minute or two out for ourselves. We caught up on each other's activities and I told her excitedly that I was just about to start a movie with Shirley Temple. She told me that she wasn't that keen about her new movie because she had to contend with an untenable situation that involved her wardrobe.

It seems that in this period of her life, her breasts had developed into those of a mature woman's and because "Dorothy of Kansas" was just a child, they had to bind Judy's chest down with wide bandages so that she would look under developed and as innocent as possible. It seems I never stopped feeling sorry for that girl and although I didn't know it then, this would be the last time I would see Judy in the period that she and I were young girls.

In the very early 1950's, my husband Tony and myself lived in an apartment which we had taken over from Rock Hudson in West Hollywood on Fairfax Avenue which is slightly below Sunset Boulevard. We enjoyed walking, and practically every night we'd walk along Sunset Boulevard for about three miles, then stop for coffee, window-shop for a while, and then head back home. One night, as we window-shopped, there was another couple looking into the window of an antique shop right next to us and as I peered around to look at the rather stout woman of short stature and her husband, I was shocked to see that it was Judy. There was no mistaking it and she was hanging onto Sid Luft's arm and looking with complete disinterest into the window of the shop.

It may seem like a strange reaction on my part, because it wasn't like Judy and I had been strangers, but there was something that told me in no uncertain terms to not approach this very sad woman. She looked so lost and so vulnerable that I didn't have the heart to impose past relationships upon her. In retrospect, there have been times that I have regretted not approaching her that night, but even today I still think I did the correct thing. How often I have thought how wonderful it would have been had she just enjoyed her life and taken a healthy pride in the enormous talent that was bestowed upon her, but I guess it just wasn't meant to be. There is absolutely no doubt that the public loved and admired Judy…. but that wasn't the problem. Judy just wasn't capable of loving or admiring herself.

The Colonel

He was called by many names, unfortunately not all of them complimentary, but even his most ardent detractors had to admit that, above all, Jack Warner loved the movies.

In our present era, profit is placed first and foremost above anything else. Therefore, it might seem very strange that during the Golden Era the head of a major motion picture studio would deliberately produce three or four "prestige pictures" a year knowing full well there would be little or no profit derived from them. In the case of Jack Warner, his satisfaction came from putting the WB shield on a production that would, in his estimation, reflect his personal good taste and thus expose the public to a "touch of class." Of course, that would be quite a feather in his cap. These movies, for the most part, were biographical in content and generally starred the superb, but less than popular, Paul Muni. Unfortunately, behind the closed doors of Warners' competitive producers at other studios, they all highly suggested another part of Jack Warner's anatomy to place that feather rather than in his cap!

From a child's point of view I always felt comfortable in Jack Warner's presence and felt very grateful for the opportunities he made possible by bringing me over from England and signing me to a long-term contract. Children, as a rule, are very perceptive in their choices of the adults that they trust, and from our very first meeting in his office I liked him almost immediately.

In an earlier chapter called "America the Beautiful," I described our first meeting with Mr. Warner in his office. During this meeting he promised that soon I would be given my first movie assignment and he was as good as his word, for it was not long in the coming.

The studio had decided to try me out in a scene in the Dick Powell starrer *The Broadway Gondolier* just to see how I would come across and how I was able to take direction. It was a very short scene that took place in a park where I am pushing a toy baby carriage and carrying on a conversation with Dick. The dialogue had absolutely nothing to do with the plot of the movie and could very well be edited out if necessary. Even though the scene was short, we didn't finish shooting it all because the cast and crew had to get on with the legitimate scripted day's work. It was understood that I was to return the next morning to finish my scene, but very late in the afternoon, my guardians received a phone call at home informing them that I was not to report back to the set the next morning, but instead go directly to Mr. Warner's office. I can assure you that no adult slept that night worrying that I had not come up to the studio's expectations and perhaps now they were going to change their minds and let me go.

Early the next morning we arrived at Mr. Warner's office, and to make things worse we were told he was not ready to see us and to please take a seat. This was not anything like our first meeting with him when we were immediately ushered into his office, so the wait definitely produced feelings of paranoia for my sister and uncle. In actuality, the wait was only a few minutes before his secretary told us that Mr. Warner would now see us.

He did not keep us in suspense and the news was good. With a big grin on his face, he told us that after viewing the dailies and seeing my short scene with Dick Powell and being assured by the director that I took direction beautifully, they had decided to star me in my very first movie. He offered his hearty congratulations and predicted a long and happy association for all of us. He tore up my original contract in place of a new one with quite a hike in salary. Needless to say, as soon as we left his office we all heaved a sigh of relief and drove home in a state of euphoria. My first movie was called *Little Big Shot*, and on its release got excellent reviews from the media and critics alike. Even the hard to please Louella Parsons and Hedda Hopper gave me and the movie a big thumbs up. What pleased the Warner VIP's the most was when it opened at the 6,000-seat Roxy Theater in New York, it did such good business that it was held over for an extended run.

I cannot say that I saw a lot of Mr. Warner on the lot throughout the year. He pretty much kept to himself unless there was a particularly bad blowup by a star or director on a set and it was deemed necessary for his

Now, now, boys...be nice! A publicity shot from *The Great O'Malley*. © Turner Entertainment Co., A Warner Bros. Entertainment Inc. Company. All Rights Reserved.

personal intervention. However, he did have one idiosyncrasy that had
nothing to do with his actors, who were always kept busy whether they
were shooting a movie or not. He was tenacious as a bull dog when it
came to his writers.

It mattered not if they were world famous authors or neophytes just
starting out, he would patrol their building and if he didn't hear the sound
of typewriters tapping away, he would storm into their offices and state
that he wasn't paying them outrageous salaries just to sit on their rear
ends. Of course, it was common knowledge that, for the most part, Mr.
Warner paid his writers scale, but that didn't seem to matter in the least.
The men found it very frustrating to be daily monitored because a legitimate amount of their time was devoted to the creative processes and the
act of typing was merely a mechanical action that had nothing to do with
turning out an imaginative script.

One day after a particularly stormy diatribe from Jack Warner, one
of the writers came up with an idea. He went to the sound department
and requested a recording of several typewriters tapping away at a feverish
pace and it turned out to be a happy solution for everyone. When they

were warned that Mr. Warner was patrolling their building, the recording was started and the result was that the writers were left in peace and the boss returned to his office satisfied that there was obvious productivity going on.

The few times that I personally saw Mr. Warner on our set was when he accompanied the executives from the New York corporate offices on their annual inspection of the studio and to observe some of the movies currently being shot on the lot. Each soundstage was alerted to when the executives were headed their way and it was written in stone that no breaks of any kind were to be taken until the men had left the soundstage, and

Scooting around Warners in between scenes from my Technicolor short, *The Changing of the Guard.* © Turner Entertainment Co., A Warner Bros. Entertainment Inc. Company. All Rights Reserved.

Visitors on the set in 1936: Lord and Lady Korda of England, the famed Korda family of movie producers in Britain. © Turner Entertainment Co., A Warner Bros. Entertainment Inc. Company. All Rights Reserved.

that included lunch time. I must say that Mr. Warner wasn't beyond breaking every rule in the book when it came to Al Jolson. He absolutely idolized the singer and liked nothing better than to hang out with him and even though he abhorred any waste of time or money he used to hold up production while he socialized with Jolson and his cronies.

Everyone on the set of *The Singing Kid* knew that the boss was a frustrated entertainer and they used to watch in amusement as he glowed with pleasure when swapping jokes with the boys. The only problem was that he had a lousy sense of timing and often forgot the tagline to a joke. Worst of all was when he tried to sing. One day Jolie was reminiscing and demonstrating a song that he sang many years ago on Broadway and after a few bars when Mr. Warner recognized the song and joined in, Jolson immediately stopped singing and tapped the boss on the chest. "Waida minute, Jack. I tellya what. I won't tell you how to run a studio if you don't try to sing a song!" It's a good thing it was Al Jolson who criticized him because no one else could have gotten away with it.

This short plays regularly on Turner Classic Movies in magnificent color! © Turner Entertainment Co., A Warner Bros. Entertainment Inc. Company. All Rights Reserved.

The big annual event that everyone turned up for was the Warner Ball, held in downtown Los Angeles at the Biltmore Hotel. It was a very formal and glamorous event and more than a thousand stars, directors and producers attended the dinner and show. You can just imagine the plethora of talent garnered from the studio's contract list entertaining the audience that night and to top it all off the emcee was none other than Al Jolson himself. As part of the show, he and I sang the Arlen and Harburg song "You're the Cure for What Ails Me" from *The Singing Kid*, and we got a standing ovation. Later on in the program, the Busby Berkeley dancing girls and I donned our plaid costumes and re-created the military tap dance that we did in my Technicolor short *The Changing of the Guard*.

All night long Mr. Warner basked in the glory of owning all this talent and he presided over the event like a proud father who had personally sired an enormous number of prodigal offspring.

In 1938, through a rather complicated set of circumstances, my uncle returned to England to live and my sister Anita and I moved to a small and cozier house located in Toluca Lake, a stone's throw away from Warners. For the first time since I was three years old in Africa, we lived in a real neighborhood that was surrounded by families with kids who rode bikes, went to regular schools, and sold lemonade from their self-styled stands on the weekends. This really fascinated me. I never really knew what I earned in movies until I was much older, so when I saw how many nickels and dimes these kids made selling their lemonade I couldn't wait to start my own business.

On the weekends, if I wasn't working, my sister knew that it was usual for me to go outside and play with the neighborhood kids. She knew all of them and their parents, so she had no trepidation about allowing me to go out and play without her supervision. So on my first day of freedom, which happened to be on a Saturday morning, I got up extra early and, unbeknown to Anita, on our front lawn I placed two cardboard boxes together, covered them with one of our best damask tablecloths, and then went about carefully choosing an assortment of our prettiest flowers from our garden and fashioned them into bouquets. I proudly got ready to sell them. I couldn't believe my luck that so many people stopped to buy my flowers. I couldn't understand why they asked me to sign a receipt for their purchases, but I gladly did so and was determined that I would pursue this activity every weekend that I had free.

Midmorning, with not too many bouquets left to sell, I noticed a beautiful limousine slowly drive by. They had barely just passed my stand when the car came to a screeching halt and backed up. The rear door swung open and out stepped Mr. Jack Warner who didn't say a word to me, but just took me by the arm and led us to my front door and started pounding on it. When my poor sister heard all this noise, she was frightened out of her wits and was further startled when she peered into the angry face of Mr. Warner who demanded, "Don't we pay this child enough money that she doesn't have to sell flowers on the street?!" Needless to say, my entrepreneur career had come to a swift end!

Even after I had made a movie at Republic Studios, and then was signed to a contract at Fox, I never stopped considering Warners as my home lot and Jack Warner as my guiding light.

As a matter of fact, in 1972, when Mr. Warner had already sold off his studio and was independently producing movies like *1776*, I sent him a letter merely to thank him for all he had done for me when I was a child. Because we had not seen one another in years, I sent him a picture of myself and in turn asked him to send me one of himself. I almost immediately received a lovely warm letter from him in which he had enclosed a wonderful 8 x 10 of himself, inscribed "To Sybil. From your very old mentor."

We kept in touch until his terrible accident on the tennis court which ultimately led to his death. When he was comatose, his secretary and lifelong friend William Schafer, who remembered me when he was assistant to Mr. Warner at the studio when I was a child, kept me apprised on Mr. Warner's condition. For many years, each Christmas, I would receive a card from my old boss and it always featured a picture of his house on Angelo Drive. Although I appreciated the warm gesture so very much, the very first Christmas after his death it saddened me to open the envelope and receive a card simply signed "From Mrs. Ann Warner."

There is just one more story that I really want to write about, even though I wasn't there to witness it. It is a wonderful story and so much like something Mr. Warner would have done, that I have no reluctance in repeating it.

As I have mentioned before, it was no secret that Jack Warner was a frustrated performer and would have liked nothing better than to have become a top flight comedian. By nature, he was not a mean man but when he was trying to amuse people, he would innocently tread heavily on sensitive feet.

The studio very often played host to very important visitors from around the world and one evening a very elegant banquet dinner was held on the studio lot. Everything had been arranged to perfection from exquisitely set tables adorned with the finest linens, silverware, crystal glasses, flower arrangements, ice sculptors, and a gourmet meal planned and carried out by Mr. Warner's personal chef.

To impress his guests of honor, invitations had gone out to the richest socialites and philanthropists and the city's most important civic leaders. After everyone had been made welcome, Mr. Warner arose from his seat, tapped his crystal glass to get everyone's attention and started out by mentioning what a pleasure it was to have his special guests honor his

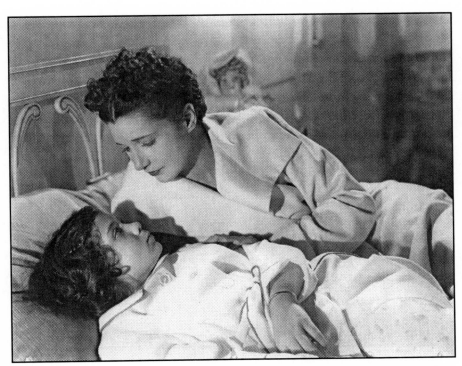

Kay Francis and myself in our second go round as mother and daughter in *Comet Over Broadway* in 1938. © Turner Entertainment Co., A Warner Bros. Entertainment Inc. Company. All Rights Reserved.

studio and himself with their presence. With a broad smile, he added that he was equally grateful to them because just by looking into their faces he was reminded that he needed to send his shirts to the laundry. One could hear a pin drop with the deadly silence that followed. You se,e his remarks were directed to the honorable General and Madam Chiang Kai-Shek of China!

If you are wondering why I named this chapter THE COLONEL, it was done for a legitimate reason. There was more to this man than just the subheading of movie producer. During World War II, his rank in the army was that of a colonel and he was also recognized by more than fifty governments, and he took an inordinate measure of pride attaining these honors.

He won the coveted and prestigious Irving G. Thalberg Award from the Academy of Motion Picture Arts and Sciences in 1958, and governmental and international honors that included the U. S. Medal of Merit from President Harry S. Truman, the Legion of Honor, ribbons from

France, and, most proudly, because he had always been a staunch Anglophile, the Commander of the British Empire, which was bestowed upon him by Queen Elizabeth.

When Jack Warner passed away, a big part of Hollywood history died along with him. For me, I still miss his Cheshire cat grin and the obvious pleasure he derived from producing some of Hollywood's greatest classic movies. Thankfully, we can all still enjoy them today via our television sets. He left quite a legacy.

Eye Candy

In the early 1930's, a man by the name of Irving Asher was the London head of Warner Bros. and as such was directly responsible for the ultimate successful careers of a number of stars.

Asher, always on the lookout for talent, was perceptive, selective, and not easily impressed. However, once he was convinced that an actor or actress had the potential for stardom, he never hesitated to send a communiqué to Jack Warner and Hal Wallis in Hollywood. Along with his recommendations was usually a can of film containing either a screen test of the subject or a film clip taken from a movie that they had appeared in. In my particular case, after viewing the act that I did on the Palladium stage which was filmed, Jack Warner sent a two worded cablegram back to London which simply said "Sign her."

In that very same period of time, a similar cablegram must have been sent to London regarding a devastatingly handsome young man whom Asher had discovered. Of course no one could project into the future, but once the actor got the green light and was signed to a standard studio contract with the usual six- month options, it would start the strange love-hate relationship between one of Hollywood's finest producers and head of a major movie studio, Jack Warner, and the neophyte actor, Errol Flynn. This friendship endured throughout their business associations and beyond and never failed to be an amusing topic of conversation in the Hollywood community for years. Ironically, when Errol Flynn first arrived on the Warners lot no one knew what to do with him. True, he was handsome, but then so were many other actors, so he went a long time without being cast in a movie. Unbelievably when they finally got around to putting him in a film it was as a corpse in a Perry Mason movie!

The person least concerned about the situation was Flynn himself.

He was having too much fun socializing and thrilling every female in sight. At that time he was being hotly pursued by Lili Damita, who was a major star, and though many had tried and failed, she managed to get him down the aisle, but failed to curtail his wandering ways throughout their volatile marriage.

No doubt about it, in the 1930's and 40's, every female from cradle to grave fell madly in love with Errol Flynn and that translated into heavy profits for Jack Warner and his studio. Although Errol was ignored for movie parts in the beginning, it wasn't too long before Warner executives started to notice that any time Flynn entered a room or was just casually walking on the studio lot, actresses from bit players to major stars, who normally were immune to handsome young men, would stop dead in their tracks and ogle the charismatic hunk. Of course he was quite aware of the effect that he had on women and for the major part of his short-ened life, he took advantage of it every chance that he could and it didn't matter what the size, shape, or age of the lady…he made moves on all of them.

I'm surprised that Flynn and I were never cast in the same movie because Warner was a staunch Anglophyle and preferred that his Brit con-tract players appear in the same productions. That did make sense since both Errol and I still had pretty heavy English accents, but the opportu-nity never presented itself. Of course, being signed to the same studio, we often attended the same movie premieres, charity and business-social events and were regularly written up in movie magazines and newspapers with our photos side by side with headings such as "Famous Brits in Holly-wood."

There was a rather large colony of British actors in Hollywood at that time and most of them attended the cricket club that C. Aubrey Smith, the fine old character actor, founded. The matches were held in a park in Burbank and there was many a time we saw Errol escorting a beautiful lady to watch the games, but, inevitably, it was a different woman every time.

As I have said previously, it mattered not whether the female was six years old or a grey-haired grandmother, each one of us would go weak in the knees when Errol was in sight. I was one of those six-year-olds, but I had the distinct advantage of being in the same profession and on the same studio lot as him and it didn't take long before the publicity depart-ment got wind of my crush on Errol. Without fail they would keep me supplied with his latest 8 x 10 glossies and now how I wish I had kept them because some never made it into print, but they were all eye candy.

My very first memory of Errol was not too long after we had just arrived in Hollywood. It was the very elegant and star-studded premiere of the Warner Bros. production of *A Midsummer Night's Dream*. The Warner Theater on Hollywood Boulevard was just aglow with celebrities and the emcee-announcer proudly proclaimed to the newsreel cameras that this was the most glamorous event ever to take place in Hollywood.... and glamorous it was. The women were all beautifully attired to perfection and the men in their tuxedos all looked like Prince Charmings. None more so than the rogue Errol Flynn himself. Draped on his arm was Lili Damita, but although he was still a relative unknown and she was the star of the family, all eyes were on him and she knew it. As an adult I have often thought how difficult it must have been to be a girlfriend or the wife of this man. It was bad enough that he always seemed to be the center of attraction, but a large amount of the time he was even prettier than his woman of the moment.

One of my most vivid memories of Errol took place very early one morning in the Warners' makeup department. I had to get there extra early because I had to be made up before I was driven to a location site for one of my movies. The famous makeup artist Perc Westmore was going to work on me, but when we got there Errol was sitting in the chair assigned to me. When Perc told him that I had an earlier call than he did, Errol leaped out of the chair and, just like the swashbuckler he has portrayed so many times, gave a bow, and with a sweep of his hand, then swooped me up and deposited me in the makeup chair. Much to the amusement of Perc and my sister, my jaw remained in a slack position for a very long time.

However, by far the most amusing memory I have of Errol also took place in the morning and it was when most of us actors would arrive at the studio for our day's work. The majority of us drove through the main gate just off Barham Boulevard and it was always diligently guarded by the Warner police. Sometimes our car would arrive at the same time as Errol's flashy convertible, but if it happened that he was ahead of us in line, we knew that we would be in for a long wait. Women, mostly young, would line up on either side of the driveway leading into the front gate with autograph books and pens clutched in their hands, and when they saw that it was Errol Flynn arriving, screams would fill the air.

Never one to disappoint any lady, Errol would stand up in his car, a cigarette holder protruding from his mouth, and would sign as many autographs as he could before traffic was so backed up that he had no choice but to move on ahead. With his usually panache, he put his hand over his heart and said "Sorry my darlings, try again tomorrow" and his car would disappear onto the lot. True to his word the same scenario would be repeated the next morning and the studio guards, who were usually very strict about anyone holding up traffic, couldn't help but be amused at the excitement always generated when Flynn appeared.

It was quite a number of years before I next saw Errol. World War II had ended and I was now a married woman. Old habits die hard and even as a child I enjoyed eating at the famous Brown Derby on Vine street in Hollywood, so Tony and I often had lunch or dinner there. One of the reasons I liked the restaurant was because at any given time I could spot friends that were diners as well as the familiar faces of Gus the maitre d' and two waiters, who had known me when I used to come in there as a child, still holding down the fort.

On one particular day, Tony and I had had a very busy morning in town so instead of going home and preparing lunch, we decided to treat ourselves and go to the Derby. I must explain the geography of the Derby for those of you who have never been there. The restaurant was quite large but very cozy and consisted of many red leather booths where the patrons could dine in comfort. On the walls were framed caricatures of most of the stars who regularly dined there and who were assured that the food and service would always be of the highest quality. Although one could order hard drinks with the meals, just off the main room was the popular barroom which was quite isolated from the restaurant proper and in that way stars could regularly stop in for a drink, day or evening, and bypass the restaurant itself.

That day, although it wasn't any kind of a holiday, Tony and I were surprised to see the Derby packed with people waiting for tables, but we were so primed for a nice meal that we decided to take our place in line as well. As we waited and the line increased, I just happened to turn my head toward the back and who should I see but none other than Errol Flynn. He was not in line for the restaurant. but was just standing there with a drink in his hands and an amused expression on his face as he carefully studied the people in line. He must have seen me staring at him because he lifted his glass in my direction and bowed his head in a typical Flynn gesture and I just knew he didn't have a clue whether I was a fan or an acquaintance. I was a woman and that was enough for him.

I turned around to Tony and said I just couldn't pass up the opportunity of going over to him even if it were for just a few moments, and my husband readily agreed because he had always enjoyed Errol's movies and would welcome the chance to meet him now. As we got a little closer to him, I was shocked to see how his looks had deteriorated. There was no mistaking who he was, but sadly it was obvious that he was only a shell of the man that I had remembered from a few years back. He looked delighted as we approached him, and when I told him who I was his face just lit up as he gave me a hug and then warmly shook Tony's hand.

As we talked, he seemed to get a lot more animated, yet when I suggested that perhaps we shouldn't hold him up any longer from his friends, with urgency in his voice he asked us not to leave but rather to join him in the bar area so that we could talk some more. I even mentioned that we had been in line to eat in the main room, but he assured us that he would be more than glad to order whatever we wanted and it could be brought into the barroom. It was incredibly sad to me that he wanted us to keep him company so badly, and when I looked to Tony for some kind of signal of what we should do, it was evident that my husband also realized that Errol's request was more than just a sense of camaraderie. When we told him we'd be very pleased to join him, you could almost see him breathe a sigh of relief.

We spent the entire afternoon with Errol but, in all honesty, I can't tell you exactly what we talked about because most of the time, I was too taken up with emotion to really concentrate on mere words. I am sure that we talked about our days at the studio and the people that we knew in common. I'm sure I told him about my time spent in South Africa during the war. I also remember Errol and Tony in deep conversation about their individual experiences during those war years when my husband was in the navy on an aircraft carrier and Errol was busy making propaganda movies…but all I could do was concentrate on Errol's changed face. I felt a lump in my throat when I realized that during the entire afternoon spent together in that bar not one person approached him, to ask for either his autograph or to just say hello.

When we finally said our goodbyes that day I just knew in my heart I would never see Errol again. Not long after that we read that Errol had died. As an adult I have often wondered what happened to a man who obviously had everything going for him, but who deliberately took a treacherous and self-imposed path to oblivion. I often think of him nowadays but when I do, I choose to envision the Errol Flynn that I knew, standing up on the seat of his racy convertible and signing autographs for his adoring public.

My Favorite Monster

In previous chapters I mentioned that there were two places on the Warner Bros. studio lot one could eat at lunchtime. Most of the stars, top producers and directors ate in the smaller and more intimate café called the Green Room. When I first came to the studio, it was suggested to my guardians that this would be the more appropriate place for me to eat, so wanting to please the big bosses we followed their "suggestions."

However, on occasion I was allowed to go to the commissary where, for the most part, the extras and the "bit" players ate their lunch and this was always an exciting time for me. Through the eyes of a child it was like entering some exotic land where all kinds of strange people resided under one roof. I would stare in wonder at the sight of an elf sharing his lunch table with a nun, a cowboy, a prisoner dressed in stripes, and a chorus girl dressed in spangles and very little else.

I remember one very special occasion when I was allowed to celebrate my birthday in the commissary. The room was filled to capacity with all of these wonderful characters and a beautiful birthday cake had been ordered for me. It was sufficiently large enough that small slices of it could be distributed to everyone.

There was also another surprise that was in store for me. I was told that a special guest who shared my birth date would be coming to help me blow out the candles. Although they didn't tell me who it was, they did say that it was someone that I liked very much. Initially, some executives were concerned that I might be apprehensive when I saw him because his makeup would be pretty gruesome. It was out of the question that he could remove it because it took hours in the morning just to put it on. They needn't have been concerned because as soon as I saw him I opened up my arms and said "Uncle Boris!" Of course, it was Boris Karloff who, by the way, was not only an elegant gentleman but a very handsome one indeed. At the precise moment when we gave one another a birthday hug the studio photographer took our picture and two days later it appeared in a newspaper with the very apt heading. "In the eyes of the beholder." I often saw Mr. Karloff at various industry events, but it would be many years before I bumped into him again.

My husband Tony and I had been married for about five years when we moved back into the Hollywood area. We had just signed a lease on an apartment that Rock Hudson was in the process of vacating and the very day we moved in just happened to be my birthday. While Rock was still moving a few light pieces out and Tony was moving some big things in, I took the opportunity to run up to the corner of Sunset Boulevard to the market to get a few staples into my new kitchen. As I started to enter the market door, who should be coming out of it but Boris Karloff and all I could think of to do in that split second was to yell out "Happy Birthday, Mr. Karloff." Well that stopped him dead in his tracks and he turned around and gave me the biggest smile. "Why thank you, young lady. How on earth did you know that it was my birthday?" I grinned back at him and said "Because it's my birthday too and years ago we shared a birthday cake in the commissary at Warner Bros. studio." We reminisced for a while and then with the usual hug we wished each other the best of birthdays and said our goodbyes.

The world is so often filled with coincidences and about four years ago one came right in my direction. I was at a paper show where dealers sell all kinds of memorabilia and I have, at various times, been lucky enough to procure some mementos of my career that I didn't have in my collection. As I walked around and viewed the dealers' tables, I noticed one that was featuring some wonderful huge posters and 8 x 10 stills of Boris Karloff. I noticed that it was manned by a lady by the name of Sara Karloff and I just knew that it had to be Boris's daughter. I went up to her and introduced myself and after a brief conversation, I told her the story of the shared birthday cake and the meeting years later on our mutual birthdays outside of that market on Sunset Boulevard. Sara smiled and said that the three of us had something in common and when I asked her what that was, she said "I also was born on November 23rd!"

Now, what do you suppose the odds are on that!

The Original Blue Eyes

The very first American movie star I ever met at Warners, after having newly arrived in Hollywood, was one of the handsomest men I had ever seen in my life. He had the bluest of blue eyes and when he smiled he was just irresistible. His name was Dick Powell.

I was supposed to have had a very small part in the movie he was starring in called *Broadway Gondolier*, but in my Jack Warner chapter I explained why this never came to be. As young as I was during my stay in England, my grandmother had taught me how to knit, and it certainly came in handy several times in my life. The first time was all during the filming of my first Warners movie, *Little Big Shot*. I had never forgotten how nice Dick Powell had been to me during the short time we worked together so I spent all of my spare time in between shooting my first movie by knitting a scarf for Mr. Powell. By the end of production, I had completed the scarf, had it beautifully gift-wrapped, and presented it to him.

I shall never forget the look of utter amazement on his face when he unwrapped it. To this day, I don't know if it was because a six-year-old child had patiently and lovingly created this gift especially for him or because the scarf itself had been knit in red, white and blue sections long enough to go around the necks of three men—with scarf to spare!

It was a year after that that I was rushed to the hospital for an emergency appendectomy. After the operation was over and I returned home to convalesce, I received many flowers and gifts from various people, and amongst all of them was an especially lovely floral bouquet, a beautiful formal evening purse with my initials on the front in gold, two dozen handkerchiefs with my name embroidered on them, and a letter from Dick Powell, telling me to hurry up and get well. I still have those gifts to this day and fairly recently displayed them on a television interview that I did for Turner Classic Movies.

It was an unprecedented honor to be featured on a Big Little Book for my first movie. © Turner Entertainment Co., A Warner Bros. Entertainment Inc. Company. All Rights Reserved.

I had just returned to California from a short visit to England, in the latter part of 1962, when I read in the papers that Dick was ill. Not knowing how serious it was, I lightheartedly wrote him a little note, enclosed one of the handkerchiefs he had given me 26 years before and said for him to hurry up and get well. I told him because it had worked for me, I was sure it would work for him too and that I would come and get the handkerchief when he was up and about once again. One week after I had sent the letter Dick Powell died, and the week following, my handkerchief was returned to me.

A publicity photo for *A Day at Santa Anita*. I was never in this scene. © Turner Entertainment Co., A Warner Bros. Entertainment Inc. Company. All Rights Reserved.

He had an amazing chameleon-like career. From being a popular
musical comedy singing star at Warners, he did a quick turnaround in the
mid-forties by starring as a steely-eyed private eye in *Murder, My Sweet*,
which he then followed up with similar tough guy roles in various other
movies. He then made a smooth transition into becoming the producer of
a popular dramatic television series and he was still active with it at the
time of his death.

I knew Dick's second wife, Joan Blondell, very well, while we were
all still at Warners, but I had never met his third wife, June Allyson, until
many years later.

The strange part of this story is that when I was a child and then a
young adult, June Allyson and I bore absolutely no resemblance to one
another. But, into my more mature years, I was mistaken for her more
times than I could count and this has always puzzled me…until we met in
1982. It was the gala night of the American Cinema Awards and three
hundred of us were honored for our contribution to the movie industry.
Lots of pictures were taken that night and when June and I were intro-

VIPs attend my afternoon birthday party at Warners: Dick Powell, Joan Blondell and the distinguished Royal visitor, The Princess of Bourbon of Spain. She and the Prince attended my formal birthday party that evening. © Turner Entertainment Co., A Warner Bros. Entertainment Inc. Company. All Rights Reserved.

duced to each other, a photographer asked if he could take a picture of us together. We did, and he promised to send us prints of it. I remember that June and I were amused that we were practically the same height, and she even remarked that she also thought that we looked a lot alike. When the photograph arrived at my home, it was quite mind-boggling. June Allyson and I looked amazingly alike and could have easily been taken for sisters!

Peg O' My Heart

The year was 1979 and Jackie Coogan and I co-emceed an award show similar to the Oscars, only these were strictly for kid actors. As an example, two of the nominees were little Ricky Schroder, years before he became Rick Schroder of television's *NYPD Blue*, and Diane Lane. He was nominated for the outstanding job he did opposite Jon Voight in *The Champ* and she was nominated for holding her own with Sir Laurence Olivier in *A Little Romance*.

One of the categories was the Sybil Jason Drama Award for Best Actress and I was delighted that the young girl I was secretly rooting for, Diane Lane, won it. She was not there to claim her statue because she was working on a movie back east, but it was shipped to her and a week later I wrote her a letter of congratulations. I am the least surprised of anyone to see that Diane developed into an outstanding mature actress and is constantly working today.

That evening was made very special because all of the presenters were ex-child stars of earlier eras. One afternoon, a few days before the big event, Jackie Coogan and myself were rehearsing our cues for the banquet show, and most of the presenters were there to familiarize themselves as to when they were supposed to present the various trophies. During the lull in rehearsals everyone took a break and I noticed a contemporary who was headed in my direction. She said, "Sybil, I wonder if you remember me?" Her face looked so very familiar to me and I knew that she just had to be an ex child star because she was one of the presenters, but for the life of me I couldn't pinpoint who she was. When she identified herself as Edith Fellows, that started off a friendship that holds solid to this day. That award show was memorable because it started another friendship that was extra special, one that I will cherish deep in my heart forever.

At my husband Tony's surprise birthday party. All kid stars! Left to right: Luanna Patten, Edith Fellows, Peggy Ann Garner, Bob Mauch and me. Snapped by shutter-bug Delmar Watson!

I had never met Peggy Ann Garner before, but I had certainly admired her acting. Although a decade separated us career-wise, we became the closest of friends from the very beginning. eg was not married at that time but soon she, Tony and myself would become like the three musketeers. I simply adored her and happily, it was reciprocated. Tony and I had a two-story home in Studio City then and we had converted our three-car garage into a little theater. Tony had built a riser, which became our stage, and he molded a series of cherubs which he gilded and placed them around the proscenium. I did my part by cutting and sewing red velvet curtains.

that could slide and close across the stage. We even had enough room for a dressing room backstage. For theater seats we purchased thirty wooden fold-up chairs from the Barnum and Bailey Circus. Tony shellacked them to a high gloss. To top it all off, we owned 16mm projection equipment with a knockout sound system, which Tony housed in a booth where we papered in Laurel and Hardy wallpaper. What good times we had in our little gem of a theater where many an evening was spent viewing films and home movies of our movie star friends.

Peg so fell in love with it that she seriously wanted to move in and live there. For almost three years we became almost like sisters, so I was completely puzzled when Peg and I would make plans to meet and she would cancel out at the last minute. The love of her life was a toy Yorkie dog who weighed a little over a pound but I noticed after a while that she was using him as an excuse to beg off of planned fun times. I'll never forget one evening when I had made a very special and elaborate dinner for Peg that we were all looking forward to. But, at seven o'clock when she was due to arrive, she phoned and cancelled out. I was really hurt when she said that she couldn't leave her dog alone and when I said there was no problem there and for her just to bring him over with her, she said it wouldn't work out and said she was sorry. After that evening, we talked regularly on the phone, but we could never arrange to get together.

One night, quite a few weeks later, the mystery was cleared up. I got a phone call from Roddy McDowall and he told me that Peggy was in the Motion Picture Hospital and was not doing too well. She was battling cancer. After I got over my initial shock, Roddy suggested that we take turns visiting her on a regular basis and, of course, I quickly agreed. He told me what day of the week he would go and then I arranged my days around it. I immediately phoned my friend Edith Fellows and asked her if she cared to visit Peggy with me. After she got over her shock, we decided on visiting two or three times a week depending on Peg's wishes or the state of her health.

On our very first visit we were very much relieved to see there had not been any great physical change in Peggy. She looked a bit tired but that was about all. After a slight initial awkwardness, Edith, Peg and I got to joking around, and that became our modus operandi. In fact, at times we became downright raucous and the nurses would peek in the room and tsk tsk us, which, of course, sent the three of us into fresh gales of laughter. The staff didn't really mind our hoodwinks because they were happy to see Peggy's mood pick up after each of our visits. Almost from the beginning, Edith and I came up with a unique plan that Peggy just adored and to which she would boast about to all the nurses and doctors when they had time to listen.

We bought a good-sized wicker basket, and turned each of our visits into a Christmas Day. We would buy all these inexpensive and outrageous little items, gift-wrap them and fill the wicker basket up to the brim. As Peg unwrapped each package, she'd give with the oohs and aahs and laugh until the tears ran down her cheeks. Edith and I had made a pact right from the beginning that, no matter what the circumstances, no concerned looks would go back and forth between us because we knew that would just devastate Peggy. That's the way the three of us played it til the very end. When the physical changes started to happen we weren't quite as madcap as before, even though we still kept it light.

Peggy was starting to lose her hair, but she had ordered three sets of wigs that she was pleased with because they matched her color and hairstyle so well. By this time, Edith and I could no longer arbitrarily turn up for our visits but would have to call up ahead of time and ask her if she was in the mood for some fun. When she would tell us that there was a movie on television that she wanted to catch we knew then that she was just in too much pain for company. The time finally came when it was harder and harder to keep up a happy front. Our dear friend was becoming so frail that, as much as she always loved to laugh, it was starting to take its toll on her.

One day Edith and I were shopping for her presents at the Farmers' Market in Hollywood and we passed a stall that had a huge variety of hats and caps. Normally, the staid Brit in me compels me to buy presents, even funny ones, that are in good taste. However, that day, I spotted a cap that I just had to get for Peg and good taste had nothing to do with it! Knowing that my dear friend had a four letter word philosophy for mean people and diseases much like the one she was battling, I knew she would love this hat. It was a baseball- style cap but placed on the front above the brim was a padded hand with a middle finger prominently held in an upright position. She adored that cap, which was never too far out of her sight, and she never failed to wear it when the doctors came to treat her.

As Peg got weaker, she expressed the desire to visit a beach. Like me she was at her most serene anywhere near an ocean, so Edith and I arranged, with her doctor's permission, to drive her down to Malibu for a few hours. On the big day of the outing, the hospital phoned early in the morning and said Peggy was just too weak to make the trip. They also thought that it would be best if she didn't have any visitors that day. I got a sick feeling in my stomach and became overwhelmingly depressed. I felt so completely helpless that I had to do something and inexplicably went out and bought the prettiest sea shell that I could find so that at our next visit Peg could at least hear the sound of the ocean when she held it up to her ear.

She never saw the seashell or got down to the beach because Peggy died that night, and clutched under her arm was the obscene baseball cap.

Not long ago, I watched her on television in *A Tree Grows in Brooklyn*, for which she received a special Academy Award at the age of thirteen. The tears welled up in my eyes yet, at the same time, I felt so honored that I had been fortunate enough to have been able to call such a beautiful and talented lady my dear friend.

I still have that seashell and every now and again I put it up to my ear, listen to the sound of the ocean, smile, and think happy thoughts of Peggy Ann Garner.

I was very much honored to receive a lovely letter and this beautiful autographed photo from the present King of Spain. He is as gracious as his parents were to me in the '30s when visiting Warners.

Actual post office stamps in 2003 in Antigua and Barbua.

Ann Rutherford and myself taken October 24, 2004.

June Allyson and myself at the American Cinema Awards. Just before this picture was taken, she looked at me and said, "You know, we *do* look alike!"

Epilogue: My Two Cents Worth

I am very grateful that the peak of my career existed in the time span known as the Golden Era of Hollywood. It was aptly named for it was an exciting and glamorous time when the word opportunity, both before and behind the camera, was a reality.

You may have noticed that my book is quite lacking in gossip and innuendo. This may have disappointed some of you, but hear this: I am quite human and do have some gripes that, considering my age, I feel that I am entitled to and am not shy about stating them. So, ready or not, here goes.

Northing seems to have changed in regards to ex-child stars. The industry takes it upon themselves to take an X and zap an ex-child actor's career right out of existence whether they deserve it or not. Some of us did not fare well as adults, but there were some wonderful talents left that did not get the opportunity to prove otherwise. Of course, there are always exceptions to the rule like Jodie Foster, Ron Howard and, just recently, Drew Barrymore, when they successfully took different directions and became talented directors and producers. Not too long ago, I was asked by the kids division of the Screen Actors Guild to represent the kid actors of the 1930's and 40's at a special meeting to discuss the problems that still exist for the junior actors today. There were only two of us from that era and the other one was Gene Reynolds, who was a kid star but later in life became a successful producer of such television mega-hits as *M*A*S*H*.

For my part, I concentrated on the huge loopholes in the Coogan Law that was originally executed to protect the money that the kid actors earned. Despite all good intentions by individuals and groups to plug up those holes, nothing beneficial has evolved yet. The young actors of today, especially those in television, are busily employed, but I shudder to think what they will face, professionally and momentarily, a short distance down the road. I can only hope that one of these days in the near future there will be a viable and a legal solution for them.

The other gripe that I have concerns our contemporary movie historians and print biographers who we regularly see as talking heads on television shows that feature stories and books on the stars of the past. The scariest part about these people is that they are generally very good speakers and writers who talk and write with such authority that their input is very believable. Realistically, one only has to look at the average age of these experts and realize that most of them were not even born when these stars were in the peak of their success.

A number of years ago, I read a book on famous leading ladies of the screen and one of the author's subjects just happened to be a star, Kay Francis, who portrayed my mother in two different movies. Coincidentally, the writer chose those very same two movies to describe the back-of-the-scenes stories and the horrendous actions and attitudes of the lady star during the making of these films. Absolutely *none* of it was true. She was a complete professional at all times, generous to everyone within her sphere, and certainly one of the nicest ladies I have ever had the privilege of working with and knowing on a personal basis. If I had a wish, I'd ask these historians to practice a little more integrity. I would also caution the reader to remember what the evil German propagandist Joseph Paul Goebbels said during World War II: "Tell a lie often enough and soon it will become a fact."

A lot of the stars of the Golden Era are no longer alive and cannot defend themselves, but I do have a suggestion to make to these historians of old Hollywood. Take advantage of talking to the still living stars of that era and check out your facts with them about their contemporaries before exploiting the apocryphal tales that abound regularly in print and on television.

I am often asked my opinion on the stars and movies of today. All I can say is that I am still an ardent moviegoer and I feel that we have some exceptional actors on the screen today. I admit I don't care for all the movies that are produced in this era, but I definitely see the quality returning year by year and hopefully that will lead Hollywood back to its rightful place as the movie capital of the world.

I have had my fifteen minutes of fame and they were some of the greatest memories of my lifetime. I can honestly say that I have no regrets

I am "journey-ing for Margaret" at a banquet in Studio City, California. Of course the Margaret is Margaret O'Brien!

because I came out of it in pretty good shape. I've been married for 56 years, we raised a wonderful daughter who grew into a happy and well-adjusted young woman, wife and mother, and we have a grandson Daniel who is 16 years old and seems to be headed in the same fine direction. Have I had an additional fifteen minutes in the latter part of my life?

You bet I have!

Nectar of the Gods, a semi-documentary starring me and Minta Durfee Arbuckle (Fatty's wife). Pictured are part of the crew, extras and to the extreme left is "kid" Chissell and a very young daughter, Toni.

Being honored by the city of Los Angeles in the office of Councilman Bob Stevenson. Extreme left of photo: Marilyn Monroe's close friend, Bob Slatzer.

Gene Kelly and myself after attending the long awaited placing of our dear and beloved friend, Elenaor Powell's star on the Walk of Fame. We all celebrated afterwards at the Brown Derby.

On stage at Bette Davis's birthday party. She's thanking all of us that were featured speakers who spoke of our various memories of her. Pictured left to right: her grandson, Keenan Wynn, Ernest Borgnine, myself and Bette at the mike.

Dick Jones and me, 2004

Taken at the annual gathering of the Jivin' Jacks and Jills banquet, with the talented
Gloria Jean and her dear sister Bonnie.

The Films of Sybil Jason

Barnacle Bill (UK/Butchers, 1935) D: Harry Hughes. Archie Pitt, Joan Gardner, Gus McNaughton, SJ, Jean Adrienne, Denis O'Neil, O.B. Clarence, Henrietta Watson, Minnie Rayner, Iris Darbyshire, Tully Comber.

Dance Band (UK/BIP, 1935) D: Marcel Varnel. Charles "Buddy" Rogers, June Clyde, Steven Geray, Magda Kun, Fred Duprez, SJ, Albert Whelan, Hal Gordon, Fred Groves, Leon Sherkot, Richard Hearne.

/ *Little Big Shot* (WB, 1935) D: Michael Curtiz. SJ, Glenda Farrell, Robert Armstrong, Edward Everett Horton, Jack LaRue, J. Carrol Naish, Arthur Vinton, Edgar Kennedy, Addison Richards, Joe Sawyer, Emma Dunn, Ward Bond, Tammany Young, Marc Lawrence.

A Dream Comes True (WB short, 1935) Addison Richards, Ross Alexander, James Cagney, SJ, Max Reinhardt, Virginia Bruce, Freddie Bartholomew, Marion Davies, Bette Davis, Olivia de Havilland, George Brent, Errol Flynn, Hugh Herbert, Joe E. Brown, Margaret Lindsay, Anita Louise, Pat O'Brien, Dick Powell, Lili Damita, Lyle Talbot, Warren William, Donald Woods, Jack Warner, Dolores de Rio, Hal Wallis, Frank McHugh, Grace Moore, William Dieterle, Jean Muir, Gladys Swarthout, Cesar Romero, Erich Wolfgang Korngold, Louise Fazenda, Paula Stone, Hobart Cavanaugh. An all-star short promoting Warners' new release, *A Midsummer's Night Dream*.

/ *I Found Stella Parish* (WB, 1935) D: Mervyn LeRoy. Kay Francis, Ian Hunter, Paul Lukas, SJ, Jessie Ralph, Barton MacLane, Joe Sawyer,

Eddie Acuff, Walter Kingsford, Harry Beresford, Robert Strange.

The Singing Kid (WB, 1936) D: William Keighley. Al Jolson, SJ, Beverly
   Roberts, Edward Everett Horton, Lyle Talbot, Claire Dodd, Allen
   Jenkins, Wini Shaw, Cab Calloway, Jack Durant, Frank Mitchell,
   Gordon (Bill) Elliott.

The Changing of the Guard (WB short, 1936) D: Bobby Connolly. SJ,
   Halliwell Hobbes, Gordon Hart, Sidney Bracey.

The Captain's Kid (WB, 1936) D: Nick Grinde. May Robson, SJ, Guy
   Kibbee, Jane Bryan, Fred Lawrence, Dick Purcell, Mary Treen, Gus
   Shy, Maude Allen, Granville Bates, Gordon Hart, George E. Stone.

A Day at Santa Anita (WB short, 1937) SJ, Marcia Ralston, Al Jolson,
   Ruby Keeler, Joan Blondell, Hugh Herbert, Allen Jenkins.
   (INCLUDED ON DISC 1 OF DVD SET 2007 —
   80 ANNIVERSARY OF "JAZZ SINGER".
The Great O'Malley (WB, 1937) D: William Dieterle. Pat O'Brien, SJ,
   Humphrey Bogart, Ann Sheridan, Frieda Inescort, Donald Crisp,
   Henry O'Neill, Mary Gordon, Hobart Cavanaugh, Craig Reynolds,
   Mabel Colcord, Frank Sheridan, Lillian Harmer.

Little Pioneer (WB short, 1937) D: Bobby Connolly. SJ, Jane Wyman,
   Carlyle Moore, Jr., Fredrick Vogeding, Tommy Bupp.

The Littlest Diplomat (WB short, 1937) D: Bobby Connolly. SJ, Lumsden
   Hare, Charles Austin, Carlos De Valdez, Sidney Bracey, Gordon
   Hart, Carlyle Moore, Jr.

Comet Over Broadway (WB, 1938) D: Busby Berkeley/John Farrow. Kay Francis,
   Ian Hunter, John Litel, Donald Crisp, SJ, Minna Gombell, Melville Cooper, Ian Keith, Leona Maricle, Vera Lewis, Susan Hayward.

Woman Doctor (Republic, 1939) D: Sidney Salkow. Frieda Inescort, Henry
   Wilcoxon, Claire Dodd, SJ, Cora Witherspoon, Frank Reicher,
   Dickie Jones, Joan Howard, Spencer Charters, Gus Glassmire, Vir-
   ginia Brissac, Don Brodie.

The Little Princess (TCF, 1939) D: Walter Lang. Shirley Temple, Richard Greene, Anita Louise, Ian Hunter, Cesar Romero, Arthur Treacher, Mary Nash, SJ, Marcia Mae Jones, Miles Mander, Beryl Mercer, Deidre Gale, Ira Stevens, E.E. Clive, Eily Malyon.

The Blue Bird (TCF, 1940) D: Walter Lang. Shirley Temple, Spring Byington, Nigel Bruce, Gale Sondergaard, Jessie Ralph, SJ, Johnny Russell, Laura Hope Crews, Russell Hicks, Al Shean, Gene Reynolds, Stanley Andrews, Sterling Holloway, Thurston Hall, Scotty Beckett, Dickie Moore, Juanita Quigley.

Four of the 14 cast members of the musical, *Garage Sale*, I composed which starred Betty Garrett and Carol Bruce. Left to right: Betty, Gloria Leroy, Joe Jokubeit, Kimberlee Tremiti and author-composer-director, Sybil J.

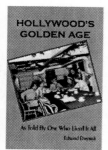

Printed in the United States
137708LV00004B/162/A

9 781593 930233